T5-BQA-137

Library of
Davidson College

Library of
Davidson College

Human Rights in Guatemala

During President Cerezo's First Year

February 1987

Americas Watch

British Parliamentary
Human Rights Group

HUMAN RIGHTS IN GUATEMALA DURING PRESIDENT CEREZO'S FIRST YEAR

Americas Watch
British Parliamentary Human Rights Group

February 1987

820.9728
H918

AMERICAS WATCH COMMITTEE

The Americas Watch Committee was established by The Fund for Free Expression in 1981 to monitor and promote observance of free expression and other internationally recognized human rights in the Western hemisphere.

PARLIMENTARY HUMAN RIGHTS GROUP

The Parliamentary Human Rights Group is an independent forum within the British Parliament of 130 members from all parties. Lord Avebury (Liberal) is its Chairman; Sir Bernard Braine (Conservative) and Alf Dubs (Labour) are Vice Chairmen; and John Wheeler (Conservative) is its Treasurer. It was founded in 1976.

88-7857

(c)   1987 by The Americas Watch Committee
All rights reserved
Printed in the United States of America
ISBN 0-938579-31-2

Bound copies are available for $8.00 from
> Americas Watch
> 36 W. 44th St.
> New York, NY   10036
> 212-840-9460

CONTENTS

i

ACKNOWLEDGMENTS

This report was written by the members of a November 1986 joint mission to Guatemala sponsored by Americas Watch and the British Parliamentary Human Rights Group. The members of the mission were Holly Burkhalter and Juan E. Mendez of Americas Watch and Lord Pratap Chitnis of the Parliamentary Human Rights Group.

In addition to gathering information during the course of the November mission, the sponsoring organizations monitored developments in Guatemala throughout the period covered by this report in a variety of ways. These included a June 1986 visit to Guatemala by Aryeh Neier of Americas Watch and a September 1986 meeting in New York between Neier and President Cerezo. Also, during half of the year covered by this report, Jean-Marie Simon, a consultant to Americas Watch, lived in Guatemala. Throughout the year Simon wrote a monthly bulletin published by Americas Watch, *Guatemala/News in Brief*.

We do not identify the many Guatemalans who provided information to Americas Watch and the Parliamentary Human Rights Group but our greatest debt is to them.

I. INTRODUCTION

On January 14, 1986, Marco Vinicio Cerezo Arevalo took office as Guatemala's first democratically elected civilian president since Julio Cesar Mendez Montenegro (1966-70). During the two decades that elapsed since the previous civilian president took office, Guatemala endured horrifying repression. The phenomenon of "disappearances" as a systematic method of political repression emerged first during Mendez Montenegro's ineffectual presidency -- when actual power was exercised by the armed forces -- and, in subsequent years, spread from Guatemala to other countries in Latin America and then to repressive regimes elsewhere in the world. Under successive military governments that followed Mendez Montenegro, disappearances continued and other gross abuses of human rights proliferated -- such as the death squad killings that were pervasive under the governments of General Romeo Lucas Garcia (1978-82) and General Oscar Mejia Victores (1983-6) and the rural massacres that characterized the government of General Efrain Rios Montt (1982-3). No other country in the hemisphere endured such sustained and pervasive political violence during

1

the last two decades.

President Cerezo's inauguration raised hopes, shared by Americas Watch and the British Parliamentary Human Rights Group, that the return to democratically elected government would signal the beginning of a new era in Guatemalan history, an era of respect for human dignity.

Along with most Guatemalans, we looked to President Cerezo not only to break sharply with the appalling records of his military predecessors but also to govern far more effectively than the last civilian occupant of the Presidential Palace.

The Americas Watch and the Parliamentary Human Rights Group monitored the human rights record of the last several military regimes in Guatemala. Accordingly, we determined to try to assess the development of the human rights situation during President Cerezo's first year to determine whether our hopes were being fulfilled. Regrettably, we must express disappointment. We do not question President Cerezo's personal commitment to improve the human rights situation, nor his political skill in attempting to achieve that goal, nor the immensity of the task that confronted him. Moreover, we recognize that some important changes in human rights, are taking place. There is greater freedom of expression in Guatemala today than at any time in the past decade. Political critics of the government face a radically reduced risk of murder or disappearance for expressing their views. Some modest steps have been taken to reduce the regimentation and control of the civilian population in the highlands.

Despite the improvements that have taken place during President Cerezo's first year, the human rights situation in Guatemala remains terrible. The armed forces continue to

2

engage in great numbers of violent abuses, and they remain a law unto themselves. No headway at all has been made in accounting for the gross abuses of the past or in punishing those responsible. Many Guatemalans remain fearful about exercising the rights they should enjoy as citizens. And, despite a few small steps to reduce military domination, this remains an overwhelming fact of life for hundreds of thousands of men who still must perform onerous unpaid service in the civilian patrols; for tens of thousands of inhabitants of the model villages; and for the millions -- the great majority of them, Mayan Indians -- whose lives are circumscribed by the patrols and by the military presence in their highland communities.

Part of our disappointment in the achievements during the first year of elected civilian government in Guatemala reflects a fundamental disagreement that we have with President Cerezo. He has made it clear by his performance thus far that his efforts to promote human rights do not encompass exposure of the abuses of the past or punishment of those responsible; and that it is the present and the future on which he will focus. We disagree because:

1) the suffering caused by the abuses of the past did not end when President Cerezo took office. This problem is particularly acute in the case of the relatives of the disappeared who are still being denied information on the fate of their family members. We believe that the government of Guatemala, and those who have assumed responsibility for administering it, owes them an accounting;

3

2) the decisions by the President to try to close the book on the past policy has been dictated to him by the armed forces which promulgated an amnesty for themselves before turning over the presidential office to him. As such, it symbolizes the continuing power of the armed forces to dictate to the civilian government and their continuing ability to act against the civilian population of Guatemala with impunity. It is a sign that the rule of law has not been established in Guatemala, and that it cannot be established in Guatemala;

3) refusal even to expose the abuses of the past tends to increase the likelihood that the same abuses will continue. Indeed, we believe that the persistence of killings and disappearances that are apparently attributable to the armed forces is a predictable consequence of the blind eye the Cerezo government has turned to the abuses of the past;

4) as important as these considerations would be in other countries, they are of heightened significance in the case of Guatemala because the crimes against humanity committed by the Guatemalan armed forces under the last three military regimes reached such staggering proportions. We believe that the advent of an elected civilian government should have been accompanied by a decisive effort to signal that the country has entered a new era. Bold measures were required to give that signal. We recognize that the continuing threat posed by the military power in Guatemala has impelled President

Cerezo to move cautiously. Moveover, we acknowledge that we cannot assert that he would have succeeded had he acted more boldly; and that it is possible that the armed forces would not have allowed him to hold office without assurances that these past crimes would neither be exposed nor punished. Despite our recognition that the very possibility of establishing a civilian government was at stake, we maintain that -- in the case of Guatemala -- it was the duty, and remains the duty, of that government to provide as full an accounting as is possible to the Guatemalan people of what happened to their disappeared family members and neighbors.

In offering the assessment contained in this report our purpose is to contribute to the strengthening of democratic institutions and the protection of human rights by recognizing changes and by pointing out shortcomings and disappointments in an effort to promote additional changes.

II. SUMMARY OF FINDINGS

The election of a civilian to the office of the Guatemalan presidency has by no means ended the military's authority. The armed forces and the civil patrols continue to rule by fear in the countryside; and students, labor unionists, and community activists have been slow to resume their organizing activities in the cities for fear of retribution. A self-amnesty enacted by the armed forces immediately before the new president took office prohibited prosecution of the military for death squad killings, disappearances, massacres and other abuses committed while they held power. President Cerezo announced early in his term that he would not attempt to repeal the amnesty, which assures that no one will be prosecuted for killing tens of thousands of civilians and destroying over 400 rural villages.

Throughout 1986, violent killings were reported in the Guatemalan press at the rate of over 100 per month and abductions and disappearances have also continued. Although the identity of those responsible for the violence is difficult to determine, in at least some of the cases, the security forces appeared to be involved. This is based on the condition of some bodies found

7

with marks of torture and hands bound, the fact that some of the victims were abducted and disappeared before their corpses appeared, and the failure to investigate these crimes or to punish those responsible.

Almost no progress was made in investigating more than 1400 writs of *habeas corpus* filed by the *Grupo de Apoyo Mutuo* (the families of the disappeared), though the Supreme Court assigned a judge full-time to the project. Only a handful of those who disappeared before 1986 were located, though some more recent cases were resolved, with several found in official custody or drafted into the Army.

Military violence against civilians in the countryside, many of them Indians, continued in 1986, though at sharply reduced levels. This decrease in violence may owe more to the effectiveness of military control in the rural areas than any real political change. Significant parts of the control system, devised by the military, continue to have a pervasive influence in many areas through, for example, the model villages and the civilian patrols. The large-scale massacres which characterized the period from 1981 to 1983 appear to have ended, though credible church sources reported occasions where members of the armed forces murdered groups of innocent noncombatants.

Another category of violence apparently accounted for some of the abuses in 1986 -- the use of murder, brutality, disappearance, or intimidation by the Army, civil patrols, or civilian military commissioners to settle personal scores, rather than for political reasons. Though such crimes may not be political *per se*, the complete lack of investigation or prosecution by the government of members of the security forces who settle personal scores violently is clearly an abuse of human rights.

8

The absence of any domestic human rights monitoring organization to investigate and report on incidents of political violence has made it impossible to calculate the degree of official involvement in most crimes. Fortunately, the Roman Catholic Church has announced that it will open a human rights office to play such a role in early 1987. Furthermore, the Guatemalan Congress adopted a law in November 1986 establishing a government "ombudsman" or procurator, who is empowered to investigate abuses and report on human rights conditions in Guatemala. It is not encouraging that President Cerezo attempted to veto this law, but it went into effect, nevertheless, because he failed to act in time.

III. OFFICIAL INITIATIVES ON HUMAN RIGHTS

a. Changes at Law-Enforcement Agencies: A few days after his inauguration, on February 4, 1986, President Cerezo announced that 600 officers of the *Direccion de Investigaciones Tecnicas* (DIT) of the National Police were being placed under investigation for human rights violations and corruption. The DIT was the investigations branch of the police, but it was also notorious for politically-motivated abuses. Its 600 agents were cashiered, and the unit was disbanded. Though the DIT was not the only security agency associated with past human rights abuses, the decision was greeted in Guatemala and abroad with expressions of support.

We understand, however, that only one of the 600 DIT officers was arrested. He was accused of murdering a fellow officer. Guatemalan Interior Minister Juan Jose Rodil has said that the existing judicial system was insufficient to bring other DIT agents to trial. Of the remainder, the majority were rehired in other law-enforcement agencies. The National Police now has a specialized investigations department called *Departamento de Investigaciones Criminales*. We do not know how many of the old

11

DIT officers now serve in this department. Many Guatemalans consider the new agency to be a reconstituted version of the DIT.

In earlier governments, the National Police and other law-enforcement bodies were headed by military officers. In an attempt to ensure control by the civilian government, President Cerezo initially appointed a retired air force officer and lawyer, Ruben Suchini Paiz, to head the National Police, and civilians to head the Treasury Police and Immigration Police. In mid-1986, however, the government reversed itself and replaced Suchini Paiz with an active duty army officer, Col. Julio Caballeros Seigne; and replaced the civilians heading the Treasury and Immigration police forces with a retired Army general, Guillermo Echeverria Vielman and retired Navy captain Clodoseo Dominguez de Leon respectively. Interior Minister Rodil acknowledged that Suchini was replaced because he was not able to establish a good rapport with the officer cadre of the National Police, and that his replacement, Caballeros, is known in the Army for his stands against the men who were in the high command in recent years.

We heard from other sources, in addition to Rodil, that the three officers appointed in mid-year were considered closer to the Christian Democratic party than to the leadership of the Armed Forces. We are not in a position to express an opinion in this matter, though other respected observers of Guatemalan politics interpreted these personnel shifts as clear indications that the Armed Forces were regaining control over what they perceive as "security-related" governmental agencies. We note, in this regard, that the changes in the leadership of the law-enforcement agencies came right after publication of an interview in *Prensa Libre* on June 29, 1986 with the Chief of Staff of the Army,

Brigade General Hector Gramajo Morales. Gramajo was quoted as saying that "unfortunately, many persons who occupy important positions in the field of security have arrived with a spirit of revenge." He added that the "Police and the Treasury Police are being mistreated. The middle-echelon cadre must not be blamed nor can they be easily subsituted .... The problem is that they try to give security through imported formulae. While they look for solutions, there can be a social outbreak."

We requested a meeting with Colonel Caballeros; instead we were granted one with his second-in-command, Miguel Angel Equizabal, but this interview was twice cancelled. (The police cancelled the second interview because Equizabal was allegedly occupied in breaking up a sit-in demonstration by the *Grupo de Apoyo Mutuo* in front of the National Palace). We were, therefore, unable to hear the views of the present leadership of the police forces about whether they are committed to reform of those forces.

President Cerezo told us that he had also disbanded and fully restructured the Presidency's protective service. In the past, both of the DIT and the President's protective services have also engaged in human rights violations. In addition, the President told us that he had removed 9 of the 26 commanders in charge of "military zones" throughout Guatemala. He acknowledged, however, that he had not been able to force former chief of staff General Lobos Zamora into retirement. Instead, Lobos Zamora was appointed Ambassador to Panama. President Cerezo said that this was a way of keeping him far from the action in Guatemala City, so that he could not plot against the constitutional government. He added that, in a few months, Lobos Zamora would be ready for retirement.

Many Guatemalans expressed outrage to us that Lobos Zamora, a prominent figure of the past regime, was not retired. The current Minister of Defense, General Jaime Hernandez Mendez, and the present Chief of Staff of the Army, General Gramajo, occupied comparably important positions in the Army since 1982, throughout the presidencies of General Efrain Rios Montt and General Oscar Mejia Victores. In late 1986, the upper echelon pressed for legislation to amend the Armed Forces law in order to avoid the mandatory retirement of several high ranking officers. Apparently they did not succeed. Seventeen or eighteen senior officers retired in December; some of them had occupied important positions, but none of them were well-known. The retirement of General Hernandez Mendez was scheduled for late January 1987, and General Gramajo was expected to replace him as Minister of Defense.

b. The Self-Amnesty Law: On the eve of President Cerezo's inauguration, the government of General Oscar Mejia Victores decreed a law establishing an amnesty for past offenses, Decree Law 8-86. It was promulgated on January 10, 1986 and covers political and common crimes committed between March 23, 1982 -- the date of a coup that brought General Rios Montt to power -- and January 14, 1986. An earlier amnesty decreed by the Rios Montt government protected the armed forces from prosecution for prior crimes.

The effect and the intent of the self-amnesty law were to prohibit punishment of those who committed human rights abuses in the course of political repression or in connection with a counter-insurgency campaign. Other dictatorial regimes have decreed such "self-amnesty" laws. The Chilean military government of General Augusto Pinochet decreed such an amnesty law on April 25, 1978, a statute that has prevented investigation of the fate and whereabouts of the hundreds of persons who disappeared after their arrest by the security forces in 1973, 1974 and 1975. The military Junta which governed Argentina towards the end of that country's military dictatorship decreed a similar law only two weeks before the elections of October 1983. As one of his very first acts of government, however, President Raul Alfonsin obtained from the Argentine Congress an act declaring that amnesty law null and void. Several courts had already refused to implement it, considering it an illegal act.

Though many in Guatemala are horrified at the self-amnesty law, it remains in effect. President Cerezo, who said during his campaign for election that an amnesty would be a matter for the courts, has subsequently said he would respect the self-amnesty. Early in the congressional session, a bill to repeal or revoke the self-amnesty law was introduced by four deputies of the *Union de Centro Nacional* (UCN) and two of the *Partido Socialista Democratico* (PSD). Others in the UCN opposed the bill. Some Christian Democratic deputies privately expressed support, but none of them actually sponsored the bill. The President (Speaker) of the Congress, Deputy Alfonso Cabrera, asked the sponsors to withdraw the bill, which they refused to do.

The bill to repeal the self-amnesty law is awaiting consideration by the Committee on Legislation and Constitutional Affairs, chaired by Jorge Skinner Klee, a member of the UCN party who does not support repeal. He has stated that the executive branch is interested in killing the repeal bill. The Christian Democratic majority has not supported it, with the exception of Deputy

Jorge Luis Archila Amezquita, who chairs the Human Rights Committee of the Congress. This Committee has unanimously supported repeal.

Even if the self-amnesty law were revoked, of course, there is little likelihood that the government would bring prosecutions or that victims of abuse and their relatives would initiate criminal complaints against members of the security forces; most Guatemalans remain fearful of reprisals. Nevertheless, as a matter of principle, the new democratic government of Guatemala should not allow the self-amnesty law to remain in effect. A self-amnesty law is an attempt by murderers and torturers to pardon themselves, as well as to impede any inquiry into their acts or into the fate of their victims. The acts that are protected from scrutiny by such a law constitute crimes against humanity. Under international law, such crimes are subject to universal jurisdiction and are not protected by statutes of limitations. Indeed, it can be argued that prosecution of crimes against humanity is a duty.

To allow a self-amnesty to stand is wrong on moral and political grounds as well as on legal grounds. It ratifies the injustices that were committed in each instance of human rights abuse. It tells the national community that there are some in Guatemala whose status is different from that of all other citizens, and whose privileges are so extraordinary that they may carry out systematic criminal acts with total impunity.

c. Judicial Investigations: The Supreme Court appointed by the new President of Guatemala took an innovative approach to judicial investigations of the whereabouts of the *desaparecidos*. On May 30, 1986, it assigned all petitions for *habeas corpus*

16

relief everywhere in Guatemala to a single criminal court based in the capital. The *Juzgado de Letra Nro. 9 en lo Penal* assembled all such petitions, and it exercises exclusive jurisdiction over them. The judge in charge of that court is Lic. Olegario Labbe Morales. He deals with the collective *habeas corpus* writs submitted by the relatives of those who disappeared after their arrest by security forces as far back as the late 1970s. He is also in charge of investigating complaints of disappearances that have taken place since the new government has been in power.

Initially, the *Grupo de Apoyo Mutuo* (GAM), the organization of relatives of the disappeared, had submitted a list of 1,367 names of *desaparecidos*, with dates on which they were detained. Later, 490 of those relatives went to the court and signed individual petitions, providing more details. Thereafter, according to Judge Labbe, GAM members have refused to cooperate with the investigation. GAM leaders told us that they felt they could not guarantee the safety of their members if they provided meaningful information, so they have discouraged them from assisting in the court's inquiries.

Judge Labbe has compiled lists of the disappeared by region, according to the place where the person had been abducted, or where he was from originally. With those lists, Judge Labbe and his staff visited every detention center, police precinct and military installation in the various regions, and inspected prison records. The Judge told us also that his procedure had been to congregate all prisoners in a given detention center and call out the names of those on his list for that region.

The results have been meager. In a report to the Supreme Court dated August 11, 1986, he claimed to have determined the whereabouts of 33 disappeared persons. Some of these were determined to have died, and the corpses were found. In a couple of cases, persons reported as disappeared came forward and clarified that they were alive and free and had never been detained, or had been held briefly and then released. Others were found in detention, pursuant to regularly issued judicial warrants of arrest. Of these 33 cases, the great majority had been reported missing in 1986. Judge Labbe told us that he had clarified the status of two persons reported as disappeared in earlier years. Tomas Morales Aquic, reported as disappeared in Peten in 1982, was found serving a prison sentence; Fernando Pineda, reported missing in 1984, came forward to say that he had never been arrested but was working in Escuintla. These results are not encouraging.

President Cerezo told us that of 40 disappearances reported in 1986, 27 persons had been found. The Guatemalan Congressional Human Rights Committee investigated some 40 cases of disappearances brought to its attention in 1986 and claims to have found 18. Other people have reported a much larger number of disappearances in 1986, making those found a much smaller percentage of the total. *Central America Report*, a respected Guatemala-based weekly, reported on November 21 that there had been an average of at least 11 politically-related kidnappings and disappearances each month in the first ten months since President Cerezo took office -- in addition to at least 224 politically-related killings.

In a telephone conversation with Dra. Flores, the clerk of Judge Labbe's court, on January 22, 1987 provided the following statistical information for *habeas corpus* petitions received since May 30, 1986 (the date on which the Supreme Court assigned

18

jurisdiction over all *habeas corpus* cases to that court): 2,377 applications had been filed as of our telephone inquiry, though many involved the same person. GAM had originally filed a "collective" application on behalf of 1,367 disappeared persons. When relatives were asked to ratify them individually, they did so in 512 cases. In addition, the Court received 36 applications from the Minnesota Lawyers International Human Rights Committee, 17 from the Inter-American Commission on Human Rights, 103 from the Mexico-based Guatemalan Commission on Human Rights, 77 from the United Nations Working Group on Disappearances and 52 from the Central American Association of Relatives of the Disappeared. Many of these applications were on behalf of persons already included in the GAM list. The court could not provide by telephone a figure for how many of these applications were filed on behalf of persons reported as disappeared in 1986.

In addition, Dra. Flores told us that, as of the end of 1986, the Court had been able to locate 47 persons, a figure that included the 33 cases reported as solved earlier (see above). She also told us that in the first three weeks of 1987 the Court had received six applications for *habeas corpus*, all for persons reported as disappeared in the preceding few days. The Court had been able to solve three of the six cases: two persons were found dead by violent means, and the third was found in detention pursuant to a judicial order.

There is no question that in 1986, some persons abducted and initially reported as disappeared have reappeared. Elsewhere in this report we deal with two well-known cases. This is, of course, a significant departure from the practice under the military regimes. But Judge Labbe's efforts are thoroughly disappointing in regard to the *desaparecidos* of the past. His methodology seems to have been designed to find any such person who might have been in unacknowledged detention. Predictably, it only allowed him to clarify the situation in a handful of cases that were evidently reported in error as among the disappeared. It is hardly surprising that he has not been able to find more *desaparecidos* in clandestine detention. President Cerezo told us, as he has said publicly, that he is personally convinced that most of those persons were eventually murdered. Interestingly, Judge Labbe does not appear to agree with President Cerezo that most of the disappeared were murdered. He informed the Americas Watch-British Parliamentary Human Rights Group that many of the disappeared had actually joined the guerrillas or emigrated to Mexico or the U.S. for economic reasons. This attitude helps explain why many relatives of the disappeared have dismissed Labbe's investigations and have refused to cooperate with his efforts.

Most other Guatemalans, however, agree that the disappeared are probably dead. If that is the case, the inquiry into disappearances should not be limited to an attempt to find those who might still be alive. Their relatives -- and for that matter, all Guatemalans -- have a right to know, insofar as it can be established, exactly what happened to each of their family members and neighbors: who ordered their arrest, where they were held, how they were treated and, if they were eventually murdered, who killed them and under whose direction.

Judge Labbe and his staff discussed some cases with us. One of their successes was with two brothers named Chuta Osorio, from Patzun, who were abducted in April 1986. GAM had filed an application for *habeas corpus* in their cases. In the course of his inquiry, Labbe located both men: one had been drafted into the Army, and the other one was facing criminal prosecution on charges of guerrilla-related activities. The latter was initially apprehended by the Army without a judicial warrant, and held for several days before charges were filed; during that period, his detention was not acknowledged. We suggested to Judge Labbe and his staff that the unacknowledged detention was illegal, since there is no state of emergency in effect in Guatemala that would suspend the guarantees against arbitrary arrest. They agreed with us, but said that no formal investigation or prosecution had been initiated against those responsible. They told us that once they complete the phase of their work devoted to locating the disappeared, they will review all the records and initiate prosecutions where appropriate.

d. Central Registry of Detainees: On August 11, 1986, the Supreme Court issued a resolution (Acuerdo Nro. 108-86) creating a Central Registry for Control of Detainees (RECEDE in the Spanish acronym). The information included in the registry is to be made available to the public on request, and the office is ordered to work 24 hours a day for that purpose. The registry will have information on all persons arrested by order of judicial authorities, including the place where the person is held, the identity of the authority that ordered the arrest and other relevant criteria. The *acuerdo* did not specify an obligation on the part of police and security forces to report all arrests and changes in the status of prisoners to the RECEDE, but such a duty, with corresponding sanctions for non-compliance will presumably be part of detailed regulations to be issued by the office of the Chief Justice of the Supreme Court. On November

15, 1986, Chief Justice Edmundo Vasquez Martinez publicly announced the official opening of RECEDE ("Establecen Registro Central de Detenidos", *El Grafico*, November 16, 1986, page 4)

e. The Congressional Committees on Human Rights and Indian Communities: We met with several members of these bodies. All parties represented in the Congress are also represented in the Committees, each by one member. Decisions at the Committee level are, therefore, adopted by consensus.

The Committees have authority not only to propose legislation and issue opinions on bills relating to human rights, but also to conduct inquiries in keeping with the investigatory powers of Congress. The latter mission is severely hampered by the lack of any budget for their work. Members have to use their own transportation, and the committees have no professional staff to assist in their tasks. These problems notwithstanding, the Human Rights Committee has made itself available as a forum to discuss cases of abuses which occur under the new government. As noted above, the chairman of the Human Rights Committee, Jorge Luis Archila Amezquita, told us that they had made efforts to solve cases of disappearances brought to their attention.

Also, members of the Committee on Indian Communities, notably Congressmen Diego Brito and Jorge Reyna, use the power of their office to travel extensively in the countryside and to help solve problems for Indian communities that were displaced by the fighting and the counterinsurgency campaign of recent years. They are, however, dependent on the military for access to areas considered sensitive from a security standpoint.

Earlier in this report we noted the role played by the Human Rights Committee in the discussion of the bill to revoke the self-amnesty law. In this, as in other initiatives, despite the best intentions of some deputies, particularly those belonging to the ruling Christian Democratic party, their efforts have been hampered by party discipline. The Christian Democratic leadership has consistently slowed down the discussion of important bills relating to human rights, so as to avoid embarrassment to the Administration, particularly when those bills have been perceived as potential sources of irritation for the military.

This concern by the Christian Democratic Party explains not only the dead end at which the repeal of the self-amnesty law seems to have arrived. It also illustrates the on-again-off-again treatment of the Human Rights Bill, which was adopted by the Congress in November 1986. This is unfortunate, because in the present circumstances, the Congress could be playing a far larger and more constructive role in the protection and promotion of human rights. The wide publicity given to interventions by deputies, and the effective use of investigatory powers granted by the Constitution, could and should provide an effective back-up to the efforts of the judiciary, of the executive branch, and of the media and private human rights groups in highlighting cases of abuse and in seeking remedies.

If the role of Congress in the first year has been disappointing in this respect, it must nonetheless be noted that its contribution is positive in two ways: one, the formulation of a Human Rights law (see below); and second, the fact that even the limited role played thus far by Congress is itself an improvement given the total lack of such a forum in the years of the military dictatorships.

f. The Human Rights Law: Throughout 1986, Congress debated a Human Rights bill, the main purpose of which was to create the office of a Procurator, modeled after the Scandinavian *ombudsman* or the Spanish *Defensor del Pueblo*, to provide speedy protection against violations of human rights. The office is contemplated in the Constitution passed in 1984, so the law, in effect, would implement this important provision.

After a protracted debate, in which the fate of the law was at times uncertain, Congress passed it in early October. The executive branch attempted to veto it, allegedly on technical grounds and because of the creation of two positions for deputy procurators. The bill was vetoed after the time period allowed by the Constitution, however. The President (Speaker) of Congress, Alfonso Cabrera, attempted to retrieve the act from the Executive, as an obvious means to give the Executive extra time. Francisco Villagran Kramer, a prominent jurist and former Vice-President who is today an activist in the PSD, filed an *amparo* procedure before the courts challenging this decision by Cabrera. The Congress eventually voted to publish the law, on the grounds that the veto was extemporaneous and therefore ineffective.

The Human Rights Act thus became law in mid-November 1986. The attitude of the Cerezo administration in this matter was confusing and unprofessional; more important, it gave the impression of an attempt to distance itself from a law that, under any circumstance, is certain to displease the military and the security forces. The Human Rights Act is a promising statute, but it needs all of the political will that Guatemala's young democracy can muster if it is to be implemented in a serious way. President Cerezo's actions at the time of promulgation do not offer great hope that an earnest effort will be made to see

24

that the law is not a dead letter from the start.

On January 21, 1987, the Congress had scheduled a session to appoint the Procurator. The session, however, did not take place. In the final weeks of the previous year, several prominent lawyers and citizens were proposed for the position, either by individual congressmen or by institutuions, and they all declined to accept it, even before a formal offer was made; some of them gave reasons for their refusal to accept. In spite of the cancellation of the January 21 session, the Congress was expected to make an announcement in late January, because the term set by the Constitution for that appointment was due to expire then.

We have examined the text of the new law. The intent is evidently to create a powerful, independent office. The Procurator is to be appointed by Congress for a fixed term, with the vote of two-thirds of the members. He can only be removed for cause, and by the same two-thirds vote. His duties are clearly established in the law, both as an investigatory *ombudsman* or *Defensor del Pueblo* and as an educator on human rights issues. Government agencies are mandated by law to facilitate his work. The Procurator is charged with regulating the day-to-day operations of the office, but the intent of the law is clearly to create a simple mechanism by which individuals can bring complaints to his attention. The Procurator is assigned the means to appoint professional and support staff and to propose his office budget.

There is one aspect of the law that concerns us: its conception of human rights violations includes acts that can be committed by private parties not in any way under the control of or enjoying protection or tolerance from the State. This is a departure from the internationally-accepted definition of human rights. But our concern is not merely academic: such a definition might open the door for a Procurator more concerned with publicizing the violent deeds of opposition groups than with investigating governmental violations. If this happens, the office can become an instrument of government propaganda (as has been unfortunately the case with official human rights bodies elsewhere) more than an effective tool for the protection of the rights of citizens against abuses of authority. The Guatemalan government, like other governments, has security forces and law enforcement machinery more than willing to investigate abuses by opposition groups; what it has lacked is the investigation and prosecution of abuses by government forces and those allied to them. The purpose of the office of the Procurator should be to fill this void.

Except for that objection, the statute does create a significant opportunity for a sound and meaningful mechanism for the protection of human rights. Needless to say, its effectiveness depends on the appointment of the right person: someone with professional capability whose standing in the community commands respect and enjoys moral authority. Even with those traits, however, the new Procurator will need strong political support and institutional commitment. The three branches of government must offer such support without reservations.

g. The International Committee of the Red Cross: Under the military dictatorship, Guatemala was the only country in the region that denied access to the International Committee of the Red Cross (ICRC). The ICRC is a Swiss organization that provides relief and protection for civilians in situations of armed conflict, and that visits prisoners held for political or security-related reasons. It is a highly specialized non-governmental organization that operates under strict rules of confidentiality. Its performance has earned it a remarkable reputation for protecting prisoners and non-combatants, and for advising governments and security forces on the observance of international humanitarian law.

President Cerezo has repeatedly promised that under his presidency the ICRC would be permitted to establish a presence in Guatemala, and he invited ICRC representatives to Guatemala early in his term to discuss the matter. In fact, previous military governments had also held preliminary meetings with the ICRC, but in spite of frequent prodding by the United States Congress and repeated expressions of "progress" on the issue by the U.S. Department of State, the ICRC has still not been allowed to establish a presence in Guatemala. For that reason it was encouraging to hear President Cerezo promise an early agreement with the ICRC to provide them with access. In a meeting with Aryeh Neier of Americas Watch in New York in September 1986, President Cerezo stated that the ICRC would be allowed into Guatemala in early 1987. In the meantime the very prospect of such an agreement has stirred opposition in Guatemala. The Guatemalan Red Cross has objected to an ICRC presence in the country. This is a surprising development, because although national Red Cross Societies are separate and independent from the ICRC, they are linked with it by common membership in the International Red Cross Movement and they generally engage in fruitful cooperative relations with it in other countries. Expressions of self-reliance and nationalism, in a context like the one in Guatemala, must be regarded with skepticism, particularly because of the unobtrusive and discreet manner in which the

ICRC works. We surmise, therefore, that important centers of power in Guatemala continue to object to an ICRC presence because of that organization's effectiveness in protecting human rights.

We hope that President Cerezo will see to it that the ICRC establishes a presence without further delays in early 1987, as he has stated. Although the subject was not discussed with him during our November 1986 visit, we did raise the matter at a meeting with Minister of Interior Rodil. He told us of the many agreements with European governments and institutions that will cooperate in training and professionalizing the police and security forces in Guatemala, including courses to be offered by the Geneva-based Henri Dunant Institute of the ICRC to instruct police and military officers on international humanitarian law. When we inquired about a full-fledged, permanent presence in Guatemala for the ICRC, Minister Rodil told us that this was one of the areas in which change would have to come about gradually.

h. Other Initiatives: Elsewhere in this report we discuss the proposal by GAM to create an independent body to investigate past human rights abuses, and the government's response.

IV. POLITICAL KILLINGS AND DISAPPEARANCES

In recent years, the military dictatorships that ruled Guatemala accumulated a horrendous record of officially-sponsored murder of political opponents and "disappearances." In contrast to the situation in other countries in Latin America, extrajudicial executions and disappearances persisted at incredibly high levels for many years, under different presidencies. Though there have been periods of higher and lower intensity, the campaign of disappearances and political killings never stopped, not even when the threat of armed insurgency was largely put down, as has been the case in Guatemala since 1983.

For these reasons, it is very important to determine whether or not political killings and disappearances still take place in Guatemala under the democratically-elected civilian government; if so, in what numbers; and whether a decline in numbers represents a genuine change in practice or merely reflects the capacity of the armed forces to sustain their privileged position without resorting to quite so much violence at a time when the insurgent threat is long past.

29

Most Guatemalans to whom we talked believe that the number of political killings and disappearances is much lower than in earlier years, continuing the downward trend that started during the Mejia Victores transition. Others believe that this aspect of political repression is largely unchanged. Yet other observers, particularly in the government and in the United States Embassy, asserted unequivocally that those patterns of abuse have stopped completely.

The truth in this matter is not easy to determine. It has always been difficult to document human rights violations in Guatemala, both because victims and their families fear, with good reason, even worse reprisals if they come forward with testimony and because of the impossibility, up to now, of establishing an independent agency within the country to assemble such testimony. The incidence of fear has not been dissipated in the first year of President Cerezo's administration. It is possible, therefore, that murders and disappearances go unreported, or are purposely mentioned as non-political in motivation, in the hope of saving the life of the abducted person, or avoiding further punishment for the relatives of the deceased. Moreover, it is only now, at the end of that first year, that some headway is being made in establishing the public and private institutional mechanisms to collect such information, and it is as yet too early to determine how effectively those mechanisms will function.

There is a rate of crime in Guatemala, particularly in the cities, and the number of killings is growing. The numbers are reflected in monthly tallies taken from the newspapers. An average of more than 100 deaths and abductions a month was tabulated in the first few months of 1986; after mid-year, the average actually rose to about 160 a month. Figures compiled by the National Police, for purposes of internal reporting, are higher, running at an average of 180 per month. Guatemalan journalists who have followed the matter told us that in the first six months of 1986, 80% of the cases reported in the press had some of the characteristics of executions or disappearances by the security forces.

As in other countries, disappearances may be distinguished from common-crime abductions because of a certain *modus operandi* and through the identity of the victim. The same applies to the distinction between a state-sponsored execution and a killing with a private motivation (crime of passion, robbery, murder for hire, etc.). For example, when a person is abducted by a group of heavily armed men in plain clothes, acting with complete impunity before witnesses and travelling in unmarked cars, it is usually a political "disappearance," particularly if the incident is part of a well-established pattern. By the same token, when the victim is known to have belonged to a political party, trade union, student association or neighborhood organization, it is often the case that there is a political motivation in his abduction or murder, especially if the social group to which he belongs is a traditional target of this type of repressive action.

The problem in assessing the cases in Guatemala in 1986 is that the two categories do not always seem to go together. There is a high number of cases of disappearances and murders that resemble the actions of security forces and para-military groups: corpses found with signs of torture, or with their hands tied behind backs; and persons abducted and thrown into unmarked cars in front of many witnesses. On the other hand, when the

31

victims are identified, there are few cases in which the political activity of the victim can be shown to be the motive for the crime. It may be that relatives of the victims hide that fact, for the reasons explained above; but given the large number of cases reported, the affiliation of the victims would probably come to light if in fact there was a deliberate pattern of abuses directed against a particular class.

It is also possible that citing 80% of the cases as showing signs of a repressive *modus operandi* is misleading; there may be a large number of cases where a clear line cannot be drawn. The fact that there has been no system for investigating such cases in Guatemala makes it impossible for us to accept anyone else's statistics as valid or to offer any statistics ourselves.

We are convinced, however, that a significant number of politically motivated killings and disappearances continue to take place in Guatemala, and little effort is made to punish those responsible. For that matter, very few of the numerous murders and abductions that take place in Guatemala every month are resolved. We are aware of the technical difficulties of conducting serious criminal investigations under Guatemala's system of administration of justice. Such difficulties are compounded by the years during which the security forces neglected that aspect of their work and instead of combating crime, whether common or political, themselves engaged in great numbers of crimes. But precisely for that reason we believe it is important for the Cerezo Government to make a clear break with the past and investigate these cases seriously.

Like all the observers we talked to, we believe that the Christian Democratic government is not itself engaged in any deliberate plan to commit crimes against any category of opponents. Yet we are dismayed by its insistence on dismissing all of these cases as "common-crime episodes" with no effort to find out the real facts. In this respect, we agree with the view expressed by the Inter-American Commission on Human Rights of the Organization of American States since 1975: that a government's responsibility is to guarantee to its citizens the enjoyment of human rights; and that this duty can be violated either by action or by omission. A governmental approach to these problems that is based on fear of alienating the military and the police tends to be interpreted as a sign of tolerance for this activity, and of weakness on the part of the government. The effect is to encourage more such abuses, and to make the government still weaker.

An example of the government's deference to the security forces can be seen in the case of Celso Lopez Jop, a press secretary of the Christian Democratic Party who was tortured and killed on December 1 in Mixco, a few miles west of Guatemala City. Local party leaders said that before dying, Lopez Jop said that his assailants were members of the National Police in Mixco. In an impromptu press conference, President Cerezo promised an investigation, but ventured that the case was "probably" not politically-motivated and denied that it was meant to intimidate the Christian Democratic Party. A spokesman for the National Police agreed with President Cerezo that it was an act of common crime. Christian Democrat Party leaders, including Alfonso Cabrera, the President of the Congress, sharply disagreed with President Cerezo, calling the murder a "political crime" and demanding a special investigation. *La Hora* reported on December 4 that 22 members of the Mixco police were questioned by investigators concerning the death, and that they were temporarily removed from duty and substituted with other National Police officers. At the time of this writing, there have been no further developments in the case, and to our knowledge, no one has been charged or prosecuted for the crime.

Some killings and disappearances have been attributed to those holding positions of responsibility in the armed forces who may be using their positions to settle by violent means, personal disputes or those of their relatives or friends, under the protection and impunity provided by their positions. Whether the victim is a political activist may play no role. Murders and abductions may result from cronyism and corruption. Even if such cases are not typically the focus of concern of human rights organizations, we believe that they are violations of fundamental human rights; and that governments are responsible for them, because of the cover and impunity provided by the criminals' membership in the armed forces.

Despite these difficulties, some observers have attempted to maintain a tally of politically motivated disappearances and murders since January 1986. The GAM has counted 128 politically related disappearances between the time that President Cerezo took office and November 15. The editors of *Central America Report* announced in their November 21 edition that they had tabulated at least 224 politically related killings and at least 110 politically related disappearances, based upon their evaluation of the circumstances of abductions and murder and the condition of the bodies. As stated earlier, President Cerezo and others in the government told us that there had been 40 such disappearances, and that between 18 and 27 of them had been resolved.

Americas Watch has also attempted to determine the incidence of disappearances by keeping track of reports in the

Guatemalan press. In the month of October, for example, there were 27 new kidnappings and disappearances reported; of these, three persons were later released and seven were found dead. In at least seven cases, the *modus operandi* or the identity of the victim suggests involvement by the security forces or paramilitary groups. (Americas Watch, *Guatemala News In Brief*, No. 8, December 1986).

During our November visit, we were able to discuss at some length some of these cases, which we believe are illustrative:

Dora Alicia Galvez Barrientos de Lara, a 53-year-old lawyer, was abducted on Saturday, October 25, 1986 after she left her law office in downtown Guatemala city, in the company of a person thought to be a client. The Guatemalan Bar Association issued a statement on October 31, pleading for her release. Her family and a few close friends made several inquiries about her. One of them, attorney Rosa Calderon, published a letter to the editor of a local newspaper, stating that because of her efforts to locate Lic. Galvez, she had herself been the target of an attempt to accuse her falsely of kidnapping a child to be sold for adoption.

We had interviews with Lic. Calderon, and with the husband and daughter of Lic. Galvez. We also raised the matter with Minister of Interior Rodil, who provided us with a dossier on the investigation conducted by the police in the matter.

Though the family has several alternative theories for the motive of this disappearance, it seems safe to assume that Lic. Galvez had no political affiliation that might have made her the subject of persecution. The available evidence, however, points to her adversaries in litigation concerning a land dispute in Palencia (forged papers were filed in that case after she was abducted). Her client's adversaries were charged with title forgery; there are several defendants in the case, and they include one former Army officer who is thought to be well connected in military circles.

We are by no means in a position to assert that this is a case of wrongdoing by people enjoying some governmental authority, but we are deeply disappointed that there has not been any serious investigation. The dossier made available to us by Minister Rodil reflects more of an attempt to cloud the issue than a good faith effort to find out the facts. There are several vague and unsubstantiated references to a possible "self-kidnapping" and to obscure family or professional problems. Though the police are aware of possible connections with the litigation in Palencia, none of the litigants has been questioned. In an apparent effort to mislead the family, the abductors sent a forged telegram from Escuintla the same day as the abduction. When the family investigated at the post office, they found that the police had not made any inquiries there.

One of the most-publicized cases took place only a few days before our visit in November.

Dinorah Martinez Salazar, a 29-year-old teacher, was kidnapped in Jutiapa on November 2, 1986. She had been a student leader ten years ago, but had no political or trade union activity since then, though her father was killed in 1981, presumably for political reasons. She was arrested at her home by persons from the military base in Jutiapa. She was held for three days in a cell, and then taken out and driven to the countryside. She was told to walk and eventually was left alone; a few minutes later she was "rescued." She was presented at a press conference at the National Police headquarters, where she said she did not know what had happened and thanked the Police for her rescue. The next day, she held a press conference sponsored by GAM, and she accused Army intelligence (G-2) of having kidnapped her. The Army officially denied it. A few days later she left the country. No one has been charged with her abduction.

It is clear that in this case, President Cerezo and Colonel Caballeros, the Director General of the National Police, succeeded in negotiating her release from her captors. Some observers told us they believe that not only Caballeros, but others in the Army are convinced that they should avoid abductions and killings except in extremely rare circumstances. Others want to operate as they did in the past. It is such differences among the military that make it possible for someone like Dinorah Martinez to survive the experience.

Three individuals in a more recent case were not as lucky.

On January 25, 1987, a farm worker named Camilo Garcia Luis, was abducted by unknown men in Guatemala City. His 22 year-old wife, Marta Odilia Raxjal-Sisinit denounced the kidnapping to the BROE, the Special Operations Brigade of the National Police at the 5th police precinct in Guatemala City. According to information from a family member, on January 27 the wife received a telegram from the BROE ordering her to come to the station or receive a fine of 50 quetzals. The same day, Marta Odilia Raxjal-Sisinit's mother, Maria Esteban Sisinit was kidnapped from her home, where she lived with the young couple and their children, and disappeared. The women's bodies were found on January 30. The brother and son of the women, Mariano Raxjal-Sisinit, who denounced their disappearance and death, has since received death threats from the local Army intelligence unit in Chimaltenango. The whereabouts of Camilo Garcia Luis remain unknown.

V. COUNTER-INSURGENCY

a. **Operations:** There has been a guerrilla insurgency for more than twenty years in Guatemala. In the early 1980s, the leftist guerrilla movement gained momentum with the incorporation of large numbers of volunteers from the Indian population, and through agreements that brought the different groups into one coalition, the *Unidad Revolucionaria Nacional Guatemalteca* (URNG). After the ferocious counterinsurgency campaign of 1982 and 1983, however, the guerrillas' capacity to engage in combat was severely diminished. A small guerrilla movement has survived, however. In 1986, the insurgents were still operating in several areas of the countryside, notably in Northern Quiché and in Southern Sololá and Suchitepé They are supposed to have a less active presence in other areas as well. In April the Army stated that the guerrillas were operating on eight fronts.

Largely as a result of the diminished threat posed by the rebels, there has also been a reduction in human rights violations by the Army against civilians in the countryside in the course of counterinsurgency operations. This downward trend had started

39

Library of
Davidson College

by 1984. In 1986, some complaints were publicized outside Guatemala, about indiscriminate attacks against civilians, by land and by air, as well as about targeted disappearances and murders in areas of conflict. In the course of our November visit, we attempted to establish the veracity of these allegations. In spite of the fact that there is now a democratically elected government in Guatemala, it is still very difficult to determine the truth about these episodes. Those who live and work in adjacent areas, and whose judgment and impartiality we trust, told us that they themselves cannot say for sure because witnesses still fear to come forward with the information, even on a confidential basis.

We do know that the Army has conducted operations in certain areas. In July, 1986, for example, two patrols from Coban went into the mountains of Northern Alta Verapaz and remained there for three weeks. In August, grenades were thrown from helicopters on the southern slopes of the volcanoes of Southern Solola, where guerrillas are active. There were also armed confrontations between the Army and the guerrillas in August and September in Quiche, San Marcos and Suchitepequez. Some of these operations have been admitted after the fact by the Army high command, claiming that they were directed strictly at guerrilla positions, and that non-combatants were warned in advance. We are not in a position to verify this. Elsewhere in this report we discuss those cases of violations of human rights which we find to be verified.

b. Model Villages and Poles of Development: A fundamental part of the strategy of counterinsurgency since 1982 was the forced displacement of the civilian population. The Army surrounded many Indian villages and forced the inhabitants to leave.

Library of
Davidson College

Many civilians fled the terror imposed by the military and wandered in the thick woods of Guatemala's more remote mountains. The Army cut off supplies to them until they were forced to come down from the mountains and surrender.

Those who surrendered were placed in temporary camps, generally very close to Army bases, where they were held for many months. The men were forced to work in tightly controlled government projects. Camp residents received food and housing from the Army. In coordination with other government agencies, the military provided educational and health services. The majority of those held in these camps were women, children and the elderly; the Army considered them all "subversive," however, and regarded their stay in these temporary camps as an opportunity to control them and to dissuade them from collaborating with the guerrillas in the future.

Once the process of re-education was complete, these families were transferred to "model villages" of a permanent nature. These were located in areas farther away from population centers, in the general vicinity of the place of origin of each group. The prime consideration was security, so the model villages were placed in areas that the Army considered firmly under its control. The criterion used to determine whether a particular group was ready for this move was its willingness to form a "civil self-defense patrol." The model villages served primarily a military purpose: consolidating territorial control over an area by placing in it a population that was required to demonstrate allegiance to the Army and to conduct certain aspects of counterinsurgency operations.

This policy, originally called *fusiles y frijoles* ("guns and beans") eventually evolved into a more systematic approach to development. Using a variety of government agencies and institutional coordination, the Army designated "poles of development" in certain areas of the countryside. These "poles" generally included several temporary camps and model villages within their respective jurisdictions. In this fashion, the Army was able to control the provision of essential services to the population, including work opportunities and some capital investment. The effect was to secure dependency by the Indians on the military, and far-reaching opportunities for tight population control.

The development poles policy has also been severely criticized as a cruel form of punishment directed against noncombatants. For that reason, President Cerezo's announcement that the "poles of development" would be transferred to civilian control was greeted warmly. Indeed, the administration of the poles of development is now in the hands of the civilian government and its local representatives. The military no longer coordinates the provision of services and jobs. The "coordinadora institucional" has been renamed the Councils of Development, and military officers were replaced by civilian departmental governors. We believe this is an important first step. It is wrong, however, to assume that this signals an end to the Army's involvement in the model villages and temporary camps.

The model villages and the camps are still very much in use and remain under military control. In the last few months, new groups of displaced Indians have come down from the mountains and surrendered to the military or to civilian authorities: they are routinely taken to temporary camps under military control. Also, some new model villages have been set up in recent months where families who were initially held in temporary camps must reside. In all these places, the military presence remains pervasive. In November, a journalist for *The Washington Post*, Joanne Omang, visited the temporary camp of Nuevo Acamal, near Coban, Alta Verapaz, and was able to talk to the residents -- but only through an Army translator. (See Joanne Omang's article "Indians Reoriented at Model Village," *The Washington Post*, November 23, 1986, p. 22.)

A few days before Ms. Omang's visit, our own delegation attempted to visit Nuevo Acamal, as well as a model village called Saraxoch; both are within a few miles of Coban. We had been told that no permit was necessary to enter any public place in Guatemala, so we drove to both settlements. We were met by armed guards at the gate in both places; they identified themselves as belonging to the civil patrol. The patrollers told us we needed a permit issued by the "military zone" and directed us to the Army base in Coban, a major military installation. We insisted on talking to higher authorities at the camps, and in both cases word was sent to the offices of our presence; in both cases we were told that we could not be admitted without a note from the military zone.

We went back to Coban and formally requested such a note from a Second Lieutenant who was the duty officer at the main gate. He relayed our request by telephone to higher officers inside the compound, and eventually to Colonel Raul Deheza Oliva, the highest military authority in the area. We were told to return at eight the next morning to pick up our permits, so we stayed overnight in Coban. When we went back the next morning, the same Second Lieutenant told us that the permits were not available since Colonel Deheza had had to travel to the city and no one else could issue them, we were informed.

We are aware that others, both Guatemalan and foreigners,

have visited Nuevo Acamal and Saraxoch. Accordingly, though we did not see these settlements, we have a relatively good idea of conditions in them. On the other hand, we know of other researchers for international human rights organizations who attempted to visit a model village in Chituj, also near Coban, a few weeks earlier. They were also denied access on the grounds that they could not show a permit issued by military authorities. These experiences confirm that these villages are still under the control of the military. Such control extends beyond the question of access by foreign visitors. In fact, the military controls the movements of the residents; their contacts with the outside world; whether or not they participate in community activities, particularly in the civil patrols; and the services that they receive.

The degree of control varies somewhat from village to village. In areas close to main highways and population centers, control appears to be more discreet, and residents may benefit from more lax enforcement mechanisms. By contrast, in model villages located in remote areas, military control over the population is likely to be as strict as ever. The camps near Coban to which we were denied access should be considered among those with the easiest access by visitors from Guatemala and from abroad.

A major aspect of military control involves the freedom of movement enjoyed by residents. It may be legitimate, under the laws of war, forcibly to displace civilians from an area for reasons of imperative military necessity so as long as an emergency prevails. In the Guatemalan context, it is not clear that forcible displacement was ever justified. Whatever the justification for displacement in the 1981-3 period, however, the policy must be seen as a massive violation of the laws of war and of human rights when the displaced are forced to remain in a given place, and are afforded no choice as to other possible relocation. The violation is compounded by the maintenance of control several years after the military conflict that gave rise to it has ceased to be a threat. This is the case in Guatemala. Indeed, newcomers from the mountains are not even allowed to leave the camps for short visits, except to work under close supervision.

Interviews conducted at the camps, when these are permitted by the military authorities, may not suffice in determining whether the residents enjoy the right to leave because the pervasive military presence, and the history of military repression, make residents fear to speak frankly. This was illustrated by one matter that we examined in the course of our November visit.

In July, Indians from Northern Alta Verapaz came down from the mountains after five years of nomadic life. We discuss their experience at length elsewhere in this report. (See Chapter IX, Refugees and Displaced People.) The majority of them made contact with the Church and the civil authorities and were received without intervention by the military. But a few days before that contact was made, a military sweep of the mountains caused some families to be separated, and four women and the children of two of them were taken to the military-controlled Nuevo Acamal camp. When their husbands were resettled in the Church-sponsored camp, an attempt was made to reunite the families. The husbands were taken to see the women at Nuevo Acamal; they had private interviews and the women stated they wanted to stay in Acamal. Before leaving, somebody in the group suggested that the women come to the Church-sponsored camp in the city, to see how their old neighbors and relatives were living. Once they arrived there, with their children, they changed their minds and decided to stay. We interviewed one of these women. She said they had been forced initially to say they wanted to stay in Acamal.

President Cerezo acknowledges that residents of the camps and model villages do not enjoy freedom of movement. During our November meeting, he told us that the Ministry of Development is gradually taking control of the *polos*, and that he expects that total freedom of movement in the model villages and camps will prevail after February 1987. We will follow up to determine whether President Cerezo is able to achieve this goal.

c. Civil Patrols: The *Patrullas de Auto-Defensa Civil* were developed as part of the Army's counter-insurgency strategy in the early 1980s. They were not limited to the communities that had been forcibly displaced; rather, they were imposed in virtually every rural community, including small towns and villages in areas with little or no guerrilla activity. From the start service in them was mandatory -- contrary to the assertions of the U.N. Special Rapporteur on Guatemala, Lord Colville, and the assertions of the U.S. Department of State -- and any expression of desire not to serve aroused suspicion that those seeking to avoid this onerous, unpaid service favored the guerrillas.

President Cerezo repeatedly promised during his election campaign to make the patrols voluntary. (Such statements make it plain that he disbelieved the assertions of those who had claimed that they had been voluntary all along.) On the other hand he has said that they will not be abolished. The President's position is that it would be unconstitutional to deny citizens their right to organize their community for purposes of self-defense, but that service should be strictly voluntary. (In September 1986, he told Aryeh Neier of Americas Watch that voluntariness applied to individual service as well as to a community's decision to organize a patrol.)

President Cerezo told us in November that in many areas the patrols have been dismantled. He also said he had initiated the process to amend the relevant legislation, to make service in them voluntary and to put each patrol under the jurisdiction and control of the local mayors. He expected to have that legislation adopted in 1987. He told us that, in the meantime, his government had acted in some places to remove leaders of local patrols -- some of them *ladinos* (non-Indians) -- who had used their positions to consolidate their power over the Indian population.

It appears that President Cerezo's statements have led to a dismantling of the civil patrols in some towns. A rural parish priest told us that in his town in Solola the patrol had always been a farce as there was never a need for it. Villagers frequently purchased the services of others to patrol for them. After the presidential announcement, members of the patrol in that town were emboldened to refuse to serve, and the civil patrol has disappeared.

That certainly is not typical. In remote areas, or in areas where there are still active insurgency or counterinsurgency operations, civil patrols are still mandatory, and they still have the same disruptive effect on the lives and livelihoods of peasants who are forced to participate. Their frequent tours of duty prevent them from moving to the coast or the city in search of seasonal work, thereby adding to the hardships of their families. They still patrol the countryside, ostensibly looking for guerrillas; and for the most part they still do so unarmed. For those refusing to participate, there is still the danger of being apprehended and tortured as a suspected "subversive." The response of the military commander of Coban, Col. Deheza, to Bishop Gerardo Flores, when questioned about the voluntary nature of the patrols, is revealing: Col. Deheza showed the Bishop a stack of requests for permission not to serve in the local patrol, and said that he authorizes most of them.

According to reputable church sources, the Army sometimes creates incidents in communities to convince the residents that they need a civil patrol, or to punish them for electing to disband their patrol. In a village in Northern Quiche, for example, a bus was attacked last summer by armed men in plain clothes who stole things from the occupants. The people came to an Army patrol and saw that their attackers had actually been soldiers in plain clothes. Yet the incident was used by the Army to justify the re-forming of the patrol in the community. Residents from the town of Paratac in the Department of Chimaltenango reported that a neighboring village elected to end civil patrol duty. Shortly thereafter, the Army came into the town and three people disappeared. The patrol was re-formed.

VI. MILITARY VIOLATIONS IN RURAL AREAS

In the course of our November visit, we tried to obtain information about allegations of serious human rights violations that were publicized in the United States and Europe as having taken place since January 1986. In some cases, we were simply unable to obtain any further evidence. This, of course, does not mean that those events did not take place, since it is still very difficult to obtain information about such incidents in Guatemala. In the following pages we describe some episodes that we believe have been verified.

a. **El Estor, Izabal:** On June 15, 1986 there was a guerrilla attack on the villages of Sepur Zarco and Pencala, and the Rio Zarco farm, in the jurisdiction of El Estor, near Lake Izabal, a place that had not witnessed guerrilla activity in the recent past. As a result, Army contingents from Coban and Puerto Barrios occupied the community of Sepur Zarco for several days. This community was formed by displaced persons who had been resettled there only in March 1986. A letter to President Cerezo from the Catholic parish of San Pedro in El Estor on June 30, requests an investigation on the following disappearances: (a) Waldemar Duarte Fernandez and Julian Izaguirre, taken by armed men on April 26. Both worked in the Pataxte farm. Izaguirre reappeared, but Duarte is still missing; (b) Francisco Coc, a displaced *campesino*, who disappeared on June 16, during the Army occupation of Sepur Zarco; (c) Daniel Raz, Carlos Enrique Cuc, Martin Cuz, Miguel Angel Maaz, Ricardo Choc Coc, Roberto Coy and Toma Tiul: all displaced persons living in Sepur Zarco. They were taken by the Army on June 18, presumably to serve as guides, but they were still missing as of the date of the letter.

The letter adds that on June 23, some of the Sepur Zarco residents heard from the troops occupying the camp that an unspecified number of men, women and children were killed in a house close to the village, and asks the President to order an investigation as well. The clergy of El Estor reported that "an unspecified number of women and children were killed in a house close to the village of Sepur Zarco" and that eight catechists from the area were arrested and disappeared. The clergy of El Estor refused to participate in public festivities as a sign of protest. The Papal Nuncio asked a nun to investigate the episode and she was able to confirm it.

Archbishop Penados also told us that the disappearances had in fact taken place.

When President Cerezo was confronted with a report of this event, he told our Church sources that he had asked the Army and their response was that there had

50

been a military confrontation; he also said that he then found that there were twenty orphans in the area, so he requested further information. It appears, however, that nothing came of this inquiry. The Guatemalan daily, *La Hora*, published the letter from the San Pedro parish in full ("Piden a Cerezo Investigar Masacre" *La Hora*, July 11, 1986.)

b. **Patzun**: This town in Chimaltenango has been the site of ferocious repression since 1981, even though the guerrillas have never had a presence there. An estimated 140 persons have been murdered by the Army in Patzun in several episodes between 1981 and 1985. According to foreign journalists who have travelled there recently, the situation in 1986 had changed. Even so, four serious episodes of selective repression took place in 1986.

The first was the murder of a man in February. Two years earlier, the Army had taken away his wife and a 17-year-old daughter, and they subsequently disappeared. The man had left the area at that time, but had returned in early 1986. Three days after his return, he was shot and murdered in his corn field.

The second case happened a few weeks later. A young man who had just completed his military service came back to Patzun, got married and his wife was expecting a child. One night, six armed men, in plain clothes but wearing Army boots, came to his house and took him away. He has not reappeared.

The third case took place on October 1, 1986; the victim was another soldier who had recently returned from serving in the military. He was 23 years old and his name was Eulogio Velazquez Xicajan. He was married to Maria Camila Chajil Morales, who was seven months pregnant; they also had a 4-year-old son. The night of October 1, unknown assailants shot through the wooden walls of their house, while they slept. The child was not hurt because he was behind his parents. The assailants then entered and finished off the couple with machetes. This happened in a town where there is an Army detachment with 150 soldiers. The police and a justice of the peace started an investigation, and collected the cartridges. They were the type used by the military. But there was no autopsy and no further investigation, and the case was dismissed as committed by "unknown assailants."

The final case is the disappearance of three young men from the nearby hamlets of Chuquel and Xlatzan Bajo, taken by the Army in August. Two others were wounded as they escaped, but managed to avoid capture. The relatives and neighbors are afraid to complain for fear that they too will be taken. No further news has been heard of the three who were taken away.

c. **Other Cases:** We inquired about the alleged murder of 89 civilians in the hamlet of Semuy, in Alta Verapaz. A village by that name and in the same province is the place of origin of the refugees living under Bishop Flores's protection in Coban. The European Parliament adopted a resolution "on the increase in human rights violations in Guatemala," which stated:

[The European Parliament] alarmed at the report by the Socialist Party of Guatemala (PSD) of a massacre perpetrated by the military in mid-August this year on the population of the village of Aldea Semuy/Alta Verapaz, in which 89 civilians are said to have lost their lives ....

We asked the leader of the PSD, Mario Solorzano, and he told us that his party was not the source of that information, and that he had no knowledge of the event. We asked others if they had heard about it, and no one could confirm it. Bishop Flores, of Coban, told us that he had not heard of any massacres in Alta Verapaz in all of 1986. He did say that right after the refugees had come down from the mountains and into his protection on July 15, two Army patrols went into the same area and stayed there for three weeks. As a result, he lost contact with other groups of Indians who were hiding in the bush and who had previously sent word that they were willing to come down and seek the Church's protection. This, of course, is not evidence that they were killed. Though we are still researching the matter, it seems unlikely that a massacre of such proportions would have taken place near Coban and that neither Bishop Flores nor others to whom we spoke would have heard anything about it.

We also tried to determine the accuracy of reports that the Army had bombed civilians in Southern Solola and Suchitepequez, in September. Parish priests in the towns nearby told us that they had heard of aerial attacks, but as far as they could tell, they were clearly targeted against guerrilla camps that are located in gullies and mountaintops, far from civilian housing. They believed that troops in the helicopters threw grenades at their targets; in past years, small planes had made dive bombing raids in the same area. They also said that it was possible that more would be known about this later, as residents discuss these matters with priests and nuns only after enough time has gone by for them to feel safe talking about it.

We also received reports, which we were unable to confirm, of an Army operation in the town of Xe Ucavitz in the Quiche in late July, 1986, in which 33 men, women, and children were killed and an undetermined number wounded. Church sources in Mexico alleged that 86 troops surrounded the town and attacked it with machine guns and mortars.

VII. ARMED OPPOSITION

At the beginning of the 1980 guerrilla groups in Guatemala were presenting a serious challenge to the Generals who were the rulers of the country. In the preceding decade every attempt at constitutional opposition to successive military governments had been ruthlessly suppressed by the Army and by government-controlled death squads. Many Guatemalans became convinced that reform would never come about through constitutional means and looked increasingly to revolutionary solutions to provide much needed structural change. Accordingly, large numbers of people began to support the armed opposition politically, and in some cases logistically, while some of them actually joined the ranks of the guerrilla groups.

In 1982, the formation of the Guatemalan National Revolutionary Unity (URNG) was announced. This brought together the four active guerrilla groups: the Guerrilla Army of the Poor (EGP), the Revolutionary Organization of the People in Arms (ORPA), the Revolutionary Armed Forces (FAR) and the Guatemalan Communist Party - Nucleus (PGT-Nucleo). In the same year, the Guatemalan Army embarked in earnest on its counter-insurgency war to eradicate the guerrilla threat.

There is no doubt that the Army emerged the victor in this struggle, though unfortunately at the cost of immense suffering to the civilian population, particularly in the countryside. But the guerrillas have not been eliminated. There are continuing reports of attacks on Army detachments and guerrilla harassment of the military in many parts of the country. Recent reports indicate that, if anything, attacks on military targets have been stepped up in the last few weeks. There are also frequent guerrilla occupations of farms and of blocking of highways for propaganda exercises and political meetings.

In the past, the Guatemalan military governments and the Reagan administration have accused the insurgents of committing atrocities, though generally without providing specific information. We believe that the actions of the guerrillas are subject to punishment through the applicable penal and procedural laws of Guatemala. In addition, without offering a judgment on the legitimacy of taking up arms to achieve political goals, we believe that in the conduct of military operations, guerrilla forces in Guatemala and elsewhere are bound to respect minimum standards of international humanitarian law, also known as "the laws of armed conflict." A conflict not of an international character, like the one in Guatemala, is governed by Common Article 3 to the four Geneva Conventions of 1949.

Our delegation had no opportunity to investigate allegations of abuses of the laws of war by the guerrillas. We note, in any case, that the actions of the guerrillas take place in remote rural areas, and that - in the circumstances that have prevailed in Guatemala - no organization, to our knowledge, has been in a position to prove or disprove such allegations.

During our visit, the Guatemalan Army for the first time took the matter to the arena of international public opinion. In the course of the General Assembly of the Organization of American States, which took place in Guatemala in November, a delegation of widows of military men killed by the guerrillas met with the President and Executive Secretary of the Inter-American Commission on Human Rights ("Viudas de Soldados," Nov. 11, 1986, *Prensa Libre*). Mrs. Mirtala Chavarria and Elsa Martinez filed a formal complaint about the deaths of Sublieutenant Julio Manuel Joachin Lopez, Sergeant Margarito Jacobo Yol, and soldiers Edgar Reynaldo Perez Acevedo, David Diaz Galicia, Flavio Alvarez Alba, Margarito Gregorio y Gregorio and Wenceslao Martinez Gutierrez. They claimed that these soldiers were apprehended by the EGP in Cotzal, Nebaj, Quiche, on November 1, 1986 and murdered in cold blood. Announcements by the Army in the first week of that month also stated that the soliders had been tortured before their death, including having the words EGP carved on their backs. Four handicapped veterans who had lost limbs in unrelated combat with the guerrillas also attended the meeting with the IACHR.

In subsequent days, the Army repeatedly publicized this meeting in its nightly television spot on all Guatemalan TV stations. Full-page paid advertisements by a group called "Relatives of Victims of Terrorism" were published in all major Guatemalan dailies in the next few days, including gruesome pictures of the corpses of the soldiers killed in the Cotzal incident. As stated earlier, we were not able to investigate this episode. If the Catholic Church is able to establish an effective domestic human rights monitoring group in Guatemala, we expect that it will be able to investigate such matters and facilitate investigations by

57

international human rights organizations, as has been the case in neighboring El Salvador.

The URNG is pressing for dialogue with the government of President Cerezo. Most recently, during his October 1986 trip to Europe, the President expressed a willingness to meet with representatives of the guerrillas. Shortly after his return to Guatemala, the URNG issued an open letter accepting what they had interpreted as an invitation to dialogue. The open letter was later published as a full-page paid advertisement in the Guatemalan newspapers. The President at first responded by stating that he would wait for a more formal proposal. At the same time, Archbishop Prospero Penados said that in the event of talks, the Church would be willing to act as a mediator. On November 4, 1986, however, Cerezo rejected the possibility of any meeting, citing the November 1 episode in Cotzal. He called on the guerrillas to lay down their arms and join in the democratization process. This invitation was later rebutted by Defense Minister General Jaime Hernandez Martinez, who said on November 10 that the URNG could not be integrated into political life.

VIII. FREEDOM OF EXPRESSION AND ASSOCIATION

a. **Freedom of the Press**: In the period under study, there were no governmental actions restricting freedom of the press or of association, and the provisions in the Constitution guaranteeing those rights were in full effect. In fact, President Cerezo's government confronted a generally hostile press. The newspapers are the same ones that were published in Guatemala during the military dictatorships and their editorial policies have not changed. Accordingly, they often do engage in disproportionate criticism of the government, but they are much more discreet about news that would reflect negatively on either the Armed Forces or the powerful business interests that most people in Guatemala refer to as "the private sector."

In the new climate of press freedom, there is more coverage of important human rights matters. Administrative, congressional and judicial initiatives dealing with past abuses are given ample coverage. The same is true of statements and actions regularly undertaken by the GAM. In the week of our visit in November, GAM demonstrations on the occasion of the the OAS General Assembly were front-page news for several days. Similarly,

59

television and radio coverage of these activities is prominent and during prime viewing or listening hours.

The reporting is sensationalistic and opinionated, and the editorial comments are generally hostile both to the government and to GAM, as well as generally to human rights concerns. Right wing columnists engage in *ad hominem* and frequently scurrilous attacks on public figures. All of this is unhelpful to a healthy and dispassionate debate about the fate and whereabouts of the disappeared and other fundamental human rights questions, but it is far better than the silence that prevailed in the Guatemalan press during long periods under the previous regimes.

In the same manner, there is now more coverage in Guatemala of individual cases of human rights violations as they take place. The newspapers regularly include news items about persons abducted and corpses found with signs of violence.

As noted elsewhere in this report, it is often difficult to determine in each case if the murder or kidnapping is attributable to the security forces or to elements acting under some color of governmental authority. The methodology used by the Guatemalan press in this regard is of little help, because it never attributes the crime to the police or the armed forces. However, if a person is reported as kidnapped in front of witnesses, by heavily armed men and taken away in an unmarked car, or if a body is said to have been found with hands tied behind the back and tortured, Guatemalan readers generally assume that the crime has been committed by security forces or by para-military groups.

Journalists do not follow up these cases with any serious investigation. In fact, most of the time the newspapers simply transcribe official police releases, which generally do not even include details such as those mentioned above. In our conversations with journalists in Guatemala, we were left with the impression that no one believes it would be possible to undertake such a form of investigative journalism without serious risk of becoming a victim of precisely this type of violation.

For the same reason, there is little if any coverage of corruption involving the military. When there have been some articles written about them, journalists have received threats by telephone or by other means, and it has been all but impossible to pursue those inquiries. Traditionally the Guatemalan press has practised self-censorship. An interesting example took place in June 1986. An article in a June issue of the *New Republic* exposed the involvement of members of the Guatemalan military high command in political killings and disappearances. The Guatemalan press carried government denunciations of the article and its authors, but not the substance of the article and the article was not reprinted.

b. Freedom of Association, Trade Unions: Following a period during the 1970s, when organized labor was in the forefront of opposition to the military governments, a wave of repression was directed at the movement at the beginning of this decade. In June 1980, for example, 27 leaders were abducted from a meeting in union headquarters in Guatemala City; they have never reappeared. (In recent weeks, exiled Guatemalan trade unionists have asked Supreme Court President Edmundo Vasquez Martinez for information about the fate of 71 disappeared union activists.)

It was not until 1983 that there was any real indication of

renewed union organizing. In that year, President Rios Montt permitted the formation of a new labor confederation, the Confederation of Trade Union Unity (CUSG); it adopted a generally pro-government stance. Another grouping of trade unions, the Unity of Guatemalan Workers' Unions (UNSITRAGUA), was formed in 1985 by the Coca-Cola workers and several other unions. UNSITRAGUA emerged following a year-long occupation of the Coca-Cola plant by workers after the management had threatened a close-down. The occupation ended when new owners agreed to re-open the factory and negotiate a new union contract. In 1985, also, the General Coordinator of Guatemalan Workers (CGTG) appeared. This confederation of workers was sponsored by the Latin American Confederation of Workers (CLAT), a labor organization affiliated with the Christian Democratic Party.

There are also several important groups of workers in Guatemala who are not affiliated with any confederation. These include the municipal workers and the teachers. State sector workers have been forbidden by law to strike since the 1950s. Nonetheless, during our November visit, we witnessed demonstrations by municipal workers who went on strike against the city government in demand for pay raises. These demonstrations were widely covered in the press and on television. The conflict dragged on for several weeks. In early December, a large demonstration organized by the striking municipal workers was dispursed, and approximately twenty of the unionists were detained. When their relatives went to the police stations to inquire about them, their arrest was initially denied. This led to understandable concern about their fate, and to public complaints about their "disappearance." Within 24 hours, however, the police

62

acknowledged their arrest and released them pending prosecution.

Guatemala is currently undergoing the worst economic crisis in its history. The effects are catastrophic for the poor majority. According to figures compiled by the Bank of Guatemala, the value of real wages fell during the last three years by 46%. In 1981 a government survey concluded that approximately half the population does not have enough money to cover the cost of basic needs. Currently the situation is even worse. There are no precise figures available but it is estimated that currently three fourths of the population live below the poverty line and 40% of families are without a daily minimum diet. Government statistics indicate that there was a five-fold increase in unemployment during the years 1980 - 1984. That rate has increased during the last two years. Under-employment, a structural problem in Guatemala, has also increased sharply. Catalina Soberanis, the Minister of Labour, has said that 51% of the work force is without permanent work. Trade union leaders told our delegation that the lack of jobs has hindered their organizing efforts because Guatemalan workers are desperate for work and fear that union involvement will cost them the opportunity.

The Americas Watch and British Parliamentary Human Rights Group delegation met with representatives of CUSG and UNSITRAGUA. Both organizations complained of delays in obtaining legal registration of unions by the Ministry of Labor, which they view as deliberate and illegal hindrance of their activities. For its part, the government denies that it deliberately impedes the registration of unions, claiming that the delays are purely administrative. By law, registration of unions should be completed within 40 days, with the possibility of an extension to 60 days. According to CUSG, the registration of some unions has been delayed for a year. Although a union does not need to be registered in order to exist, it is not a legal entity until registration is completed and cannot, for example, obtain banking credit or make legal representation to the courts.

While the government does not place restrictions on association, movement, or speech in urban areas, trade unionists have complained that employers impede the organization of workers by making jobs conditional on assurances that unions will not be formed. The labor confederations are currently protesting several instances of lay-offs for union activity; but in other cases, the workers themselves have asked the unions not to proceed with cases, for fear of retribution. Labor leaders also told us that organizing is very difficult because of the fear instilled in workers by years of very brutal repression against any and all trade union activity. Their rank-and-file and potential activists simply do not believe it is safe in Guatemala to engage in open trade union activity. Union leaders themselves are subjected to such petty harassment as receiving requests to make legal statements at odd hours, or inquiries by strangers at their homes, or the homes of friends and relatives.

By far the most serious issue raised by trade unionists are instances of violence that continue against labor activists. Although such violations do not approach the level of the early 1980s, occasional killings and abductions serve as reminders of a period when union activity was all but extinguished, and inhibit organizing and recruitment by terrifying other workers.

In February, 1986, Jose Mercedes Sotz of the Municipal Workers Union, who had been protesting lay-offs, was abducted and held for several days. After his release he accused the bodyguards of the Mayor of Guatemala City of kidnapping him and

64

claimed that he had been beaten during the time he was held. On May 31, the three-year-old son of Mercedes Sotz was shot in the back, while walking in Guatemala City with his father.

On July 23, 1986, Justo Rufino Reyes Alvarado, the 53-year-old Secretary for Social Welfare of the Central Union for Municipal Workers was stabbed to death. According to a report in *El Grafico*, July 24, the victim's documents and money were not stolen. Christian Democrat (DCG) Congressman, Otto Baechli, stated that "The victim's position in the city union indicates it was politically motivated", and DCG Congressman Alfonso Alonzo said that "it is certain that the government is incapable of controlling violence... we must accept the fact that we have a police administration with antidemocratic procedures". (*La Hora*, July 24.)

Representatives of the Cerezo Government admitted privately that this was a politically-motivated crime, and promised an investigation. The State Department claimed that in fact the murder had been caused by internal squabbles within the union movement, and that the security forces were not involved. Trade unionists we interviewed in Guatemala insisted that Reyes's death was a clear-cut case of political murder. The police announced that, in connection with Mr. Reyes's murder, they were looking for a fellow trade union activist, Catalino Godinez Morales. In August, Mr. Godinez Morales was found dead; we do not know whether the police had apprehended him before his death.

On October 23, 1986, Edilio Viera Guzman, Secretary General of the Street Vendors Union, a CUSG affiliate, was abducted, stabbed and killed in the same manner as Reyes. CUSG officials made representations to the police about the case and were told that a formal complaint, signed by the Secretary

General, Francisco Alfaro, was necessary. CUSG did not make such a complaint, fearing the risks involved.

On November 14, Juan Manual Valazquez, a leader of the municipal workers of Guatemala City who were on strike at the time, disappeared on his way home from participating in the strike action. He was found unconscious and badly beaten on the outskirts of the city, several days later. On November 15, 75 municipal workers were dismissed by the Mayor of Guatemala City, Alvaro Arzu. The union denounced the dismissals as intimidation.

Other labor protest actions have been inhibited. The *Sindicato de Trabajadores de la Universidad de San Carlos* (STUSC) which represents the groundskeepers and administrative employees at Guatemala's largest university, took over some campus buildings in the course of a labor conflict with the authorities. Some leaders were formally charged with kidnapping (because of the presence of non-demonstrators on the premises) and prosecuted.

In rural areas, union conflicts have been treated similarly, and perhaps with more violence. We heard of cases in which local peasant leaders have been assaulted, presumably by thugs in the service of landowners, in an effort to discourage them from pressing their demands.

c. The Grupo de Apoyo Mutuo (GAM): In the year covered by this report, the GAM asserted itself as an independent human rights organization, the first of its kind to operate in Guatemala in many years. Under Mejia Victores, the GAM survived serious challenges to its very existence, including direct personal threats to many of its members, and the murder of two of its leaders in

66

March and April 1985. Others in the founding group eventually were forced into exile, but the GAM never stopped pressing for an accounting of the fate and whereabouts of the disappeared. (See the Americas Watch report, "Guatemala: The Group for Mutual Support," New York, November 1985.)

Because of its perseverance and courage, the GAM enjoys considerable prestige and recognition, as well as the support of many community-based organizations and individuals in Guatemala. At the same time, it has benefited from support from human rights organizations, churches and institutions in democratic countries throughout the world. In December 1986, GAM was given the prestigious Carter-De Menil Human Rights Award at a ceremony in Houston, Texas. In 1986, also, it was nominated by British members of Parliament for the Nobel Peace Prize.

During 1986, GAM succeeded in publicizing the issue of the disappeared and making it a high priority in the national debate. Even before the inauguration, GAM demanded and obtained from President-elect Cerezo a commitment to investigate the fate and whereabouts of the disappeared. In the first few weeks of the Cerezo administration, the government announced that it would create a commission to investigate disappearances.

Also, as noted above, GAM filed an application for *habeas corpus* on behalf of some 1,367 persons who had disappeared after their arrest by security forces. Other petitions were filed by individual relatives and by a United States human rights organization, the Minnesota Lawyers International Human Rights Committee. As reported above, the Supreme Court appointed one judge in the criminal division to hear all *habeas corpus* petitions. Citing the consideration of disappearances by the courts, President Cerezo reversed a decision to create a special commission, stating that its establishment creation would interfere with the work of the judiciary.

GAM disagreed, and continued to insist on the creation of an investigatory body. In the meantime, it cooperated initially with Judge Labbe's work, by having around 500 of its members go to the courthouse and ratify their petitions individually. Later GAM decided to withdraw that support on the grounds that no one was willing to offer guarantees for the safety of those relatives who might present evidence.

In September, GAM staged a non-violent protest demanding a decision by Cerezo to form the special commission. The protest consisted of sitting in the President's waiting room until he received the GAM delegation. The police forcibly removed the demonstrators from the offices of the Presidency. Also in September, GAM demonstrators marched during a military parade, following columns from the Army and shouting hostile chants. In November, GAM organized several demonstrations in connection with the OAS General Assembly meeting in Guatemala. In the same week, it staged a demonstration at the gate of the Presidential Palace, demanding an interview with the President. On the second day, the GAM members were forcibly removed from the Palace doors, and they continued their vigil, for a total of 60 hours, in the square across the street from the Palace.

During our November visit, we were able to witness these demonstrations, and were impressed by the self-discipline and determination exhibited by every one in the large group. At certain hours of the night, the group was the target of hostile verbal attacks from passing cars; on the other hand, we were also able to see many demonstrations of spontaneous support from passersby. When the police were called in to remove them, GAM members used civil disobedience techniques. In forcibly ejecting them, the police sometimes used excessive force, producing bruises and concussions.

As a result of the November episodes, Minister of Interior Juan Jose Rodil announced that demonstrations by GAM in public buildings would not be tolerated, and that steps would be taken to expel non-Guatemalan supporters of the movement called Peace Brigades International (PBI) who participated in the demonstrations. PBI has a large presence in Guatemala, mostly of young persons from Europe and North America, who lend permanent support and assistance to GAM. (Since the murder of two GAM leaders in March and April 1985, PBI members have accompanied surviving GAM leaders at all hours of the day and night to provide them unarmed protection.) Many of these young people participate in GAM marches and demonstrations. During the November vigil, some of them tried to stand between the police and the demonstrators, thus making their ejection more difficult. As far as we know, this threat of deportation has not been carried out. In our view, it would set a bad precedent for the Guatemalan government to take such a drastic measure as expulsion for the relatively minor breach of the law that might be involved in participating in a non-violent demonstration for human rights.

In its debate with the President, (conducted mostly through the communications media), GAM insisted that the commission should include well-known personalities from Guatemala and from other countries, suggesting the names of representatives of mass-based organizations and internationally-known human rights leaders such as Nobel Peace Laureate Adolfo Perez Esquivel and

69

Spanish human rights lawyer Antonio Garcia Borrajo.

In December 1986 and in January 1987, President Cerezo stated that he had decided to appoint the commission, again reversing an earlier decision, and that the persons to be appointed to it would be named in February 1987. He rejected the notion of including non-Guatemalans, or citizens representing trade unions or other bodies. Though he asserted that the commission would be a part of the executive branch, he did not elaborate as to its powers and mandate.

In December, GAM announced the disappearance of Mr. Basilio Tuiz Ramirez, 28, the brother of a GAM member. Another brother of the family is among the disappeared. Basilio Tuiz Ramirez was a leader of the community in Santiago Atitlan, Solola. According to GAM's information, he received a bullet wound on December 18 in Panul, near Santiago Atitlan, when unknown assailants attempted to abduct him. Doctors in Santiago Atitlan refused to treat him, presumably for fear of reprisals. He was captured in front of witnesses the next day, when he was being taken to a hospital in Solola. The office of the Presidency stated that he could have been wounded in a confrontation between the guerrillas and the Army because such confrontations did take place in that area at that time. The family strongly denied such a possibility. The government has not provided any information about his whereabouts, nor has it admitted that he was arrested. On December 27, the Defense Ministry denied that the Army had played any role in the case, and attributed the accusation to "a disinformation campaign about the Army." (press communique, FBIS, 29-Dec-86, page P-3). As of January 6, 1987, the fate and whereabouts of Mr. Tuiz had not been established.

The announcement by the office of the Presidency about the possibility of a confrontation is very disappointing. It does nothing to clarify the legal status of the person, and it seems designed to create the impression that Mr. Tuiz might have been involved in armed opposition to the government. If that is the case, then the government should offer the evidence and bring Mr. Tuiz to justice. If the government has no such evidence, the statement is a shameful aspersion cast on someone who is obviously not in a position to defend himself. Moreover, it seems designed to sow doubt in public opinion about the information provided by his relatives and by GAM without offering more precise and reliable information. Whatever the intent of such a comment, it is no substitute for the government's obligation to investigate the matter thoroughly and diligently. As far as we know, such an investigation has not taken place as of this writing.

IX. REFUGEES AND DISPLACED PEOPLE

The situation of refugees and of those displaced within Guatemala illustrates the military's continued control over rural areas and the difficulties which the civilian government faces in providing security and stability for returned refugees and resettled civilians.

a. The Internally Displaced: Exact figures on the number of Guatemalans displaced from their homes by the war are not available, though church sources estimated in 1982 and 1983 that there were as many as one million. Scores of thousands fled to the slums of Guatemala City where they live in hopeless misery. Infant mortality is high and such diseases as typhoid are prevalent. Catholic clergy who work with the displaced in Guatemala City informed the Americas Watch/Parliamentary Human Rights Group November delegation that the displaced population has stabilized in the past year and that large numbers are no longer fleeing Army operations in the countryside, as in the early 1980s. Nonetheless, the displaced still fear the Army; many lack identity documents and do not apply for new ones because they fear revealing their towns of origin. Almost all the Indians who have come to Guatemala City have abandoned their traditional dress for fear of identification by the authorities; many still prevent their children from attending school for the same reason.

The Americas Watch/British Parliamentary Human Rights Group delegation met with members of CONFREGUA, a federation of religious orders in Guatemala, who work extensively with the displaced in Guatemala City. We were told that in the first six months of 1986, the major problem facing displaced people in the urban areas was violence. They estimate that at least 15 killings or disappearances have taken place since January 1986 among this sector. In the last half of the year the violence was less and economic hardship was the most serious difficulty the displaced faced.

In rural areas, tens of thousands of displaced peasants have been collected into Army-built model villages, where many are completely dependent upon inadequate relief handouts and jobs. With the election of the civilian government, the Army has stopped supplying food and building materials in many communities, stating that it is the civilian government's responsibility. The civilian government has not been able to meet the need, however, and hunger, disease and unemployment are common. Elsewhere, the civilian government actually appears to compete with the Army in promoting development. Guatemalan journalists informed the delegation that the Army has hired some 1,500 "social promoters" to work in rural areas, implementing the Army's program of winning hearts and minds. The Cerezo Government, for its part, has hired 500 promoters; at the time of our November visit, we were informed that the civilian promoters were still in training and not yet in the field.

74

Throughout the past year, the Army's public relations office has reported that groups of internally displaced people were "turning themselves in" to local Army bases. In the past, civilians fleeing conflict zones were considered by the Army to be guerrillas themselves, and some of those who were captured were killed. Others who turned themselves in because they were starving in the mountains after being forced to flee their villages were first sent to re-education camps and then settled in model villages. Under the Cerezo government, the Army has maintained the latter practice, and "forgives" displaced civilians for alleged past association with the guerrillas and installs them in model villages, or permits them to return to their former villages. (Many of the displaced cannot return to their own villages, however, because they have been destroyed; the Army itself released the figure of 440 villages which were completely destroyed during the Army's counterinsurgency war in the countryside.) In June 1986, for example, the press reported that three groups of the internally displaced, totaling 136 people, including 112 women and children, had "turned themselves in" to the Army -- which announced its intention of settling them in a model village.

The Army continues to maintain several special facilities for reception and "re-education" of the displaced. While no new re-education camps have been built since President Cerezo took office, new groups of the internally displaced entered existing facilities throughout his first year in office.

In addition to those who have come down from the mountains and sought food and housing from military or civilian authorities, unknown numbers of the displaced still roam the mountainous highlands. Although they fear the Army and do not want to live in development poles, their own villages and homes are gone, and they are unable to work or plant crops. One such group, including 107 Kekchi Indian men, women, and children, had been wandering in the mountains outside Coban in Alta Verapaz since 1981, when an Army massacre drove them from their village. In 1986, the group heard reports of a new government which promised an end to military violence. In June, their leader, Juan Tum Cho, sent word to the Bishop of Coban, Monsignor Gerardo Flores Reyes, that they wished to surrender to him. With the help of the Christian Democrat Departmental Governor, Juan de Dios Martinez, who promised to "override the local military command who demand that the refugees be turned over for internment in one of their model villages" the Bishop received the group and installed them in an abandoned hospital in Coban. Just three hours after the rendezvous, two patrols of soldiers occupied the area and captured 75 additional displaced people who were then sent to an Army re-education camp, Acamal. (Bishop Flores, who had been contacted by other groups of homeless Kekchis wandering in the mountains, subsequently lost all contact with them, and told our November delegation that he fears that the Army's recent operations have frightened them into flight.) The local military commander has repeatedly requested that the Bishop turn over to the Army this group -- that is, those who surrendered to the Bishop -- whom the commander refers to as "subversives." Meanwhile, President Cerezo has taken an interest in the group and has promised them a plot of land in the neighboring department of Quiche. Yet Bishop Flores does not consider it safe for the Indians to leave his protection. He informed our delegation that, earlier in the year, without involving the civilian government he had attempted to resettle a group of 23 dislaced Indians who came down from the mountains. Following the abduction and disappearance of two of the men, however, he abandoned the effort to keep the group together, and dispersed them about the community.

As mentioned elsewhere in this report, another case of a group of the displaced "turning themselves in" to the Army at about the same time had tragic consequences. According to local church sources from the San Pedro parish in El Estor, in the eastern department of Izabal, the military apparently abducted eight catechists from a group of displaced persons who were relocated in the community of Sepur Zarco.

b. Repatriation of Refugees: Estimates of the number of Guatemalan refugees living in Mexico vary, but according to the Mexican Government's Commission for Assistance to Refugees (COMAR) there are as many as 200,000 Guatemalans in Mexico, including some 40,000 living in refugee camps as well as the much larger number of "unofficial" refugees not living in recognized camps. (*Uno Mas Uno*, August 28, 1985.) The Cerezo Government considers the repatriation of the refugees from Mexico a matter of national pride, and has started negotiations which are continuing, with the UNHCR and the Government of Mexico regarding their return. Nonetheless, President Cerezo recognizes the risks to the refugees upon their return, and the government is moving slowly in this area. While publicly urging the refugees to return, President Cerezo told church sources during a July 1986 visit to Mexico that repatriation of refugees from Mexico cannot take place until 1987 as circumstances in Guatemala did not yet guarantee their safety or freedom.

77

Christian Democrat Secretary General Cabrera Hidalgo also cautioned the refugees against returning too soon, noting that "After 30 years of the permanent violation of the law, repression and dictatorship, it is not easy to change things in one month... or five." (*El Grafico*, February 22, 1986.)

The Army apparently considers those who fled the country to be guerrillas or, at least, guerrilla sympathizers. In 1983, for example, Guatemalan Army soldiers crossed the border into Mexico, raiding and looting camps and killing refugees. Though such attacks have ended, as recently as June 1986 Defense Minister Hernandez claimed that the refugee camps in Chiapas Mexico were guerrilla bases.

Given the continuing evidence of Army hostility toward the refugees, few refugees have returned to Guatemala during President Cerezo's first year in office. According to the United Nations High Commissioner for Refugees (UNHCR), as of October 1986, a total of 1042 refugees in Mexico had returned since 1984, including 343 who arrived in 1986.

In a letter to President Cerezo in July, a group of Guatemalan refugees in Mexico stated that "We will not return to Guatemala because the peasants' killers are still roaming freely." The authors of the letter said that conditions for their return would be the punishment of those responsible for massacres, return of their land, elimination of the civil patrols, and indemnification for damages. (*El Grafico*, July 2, 1986)

President Cerezo has stated that "if someone has nowhere to go because of his loss [of home and land], he can solicit aid in a Development Pole." (*Diario de Centro America*, March 10, 1986) In his November 13 meeting with the Americas Watch/ Parliamentary Human Rights Group delegation, President Cerezo stressed that he welcomed the return of the refugees and the assistance of the UNHCR in facilitating repatriation, and insisted that the government did not tell the returnees where they must live. The president cited a case of refugees returning to the Quiche whom he warned against settling in a particular area due to the presence of guerrillas. Nonetheless, he said, the refugees went their own way without interference, though the group later returned to the town of La Perla seeking government assistance. While there does not appear to be a government policy of forcing returning refugees to live in model villages, the absence of civilian government programs for those whose homes, villages, and crops were destroyed by the Army under previous governments limits the options of the returnees.

In addition to the thousands of Guatemalans in Mexico, there is a group of some 6,800 Kanjobal Indian refugees living in Florida and California. In mid-June, an alternate Congressman from the Christian Democrat party, Jorge Reyna Castillo, visited the U.S. and stated that the Indians are "thinking of returning to Guatemala" but they are demanding that first, they not be forced to live in model villages, and second, "that they don't have to get mixed up in the civil patrols." (Siete Dias TV news, June 10).

X. U.S. POLICY TOWARDS GUATEMALA:
REMARKS BY THE AMERICAS WATCH

The election of a civilian to the presidency of Guatemala is an important first step in a process of restoring democracy and protecting human rights in a country long ruled by military dictatorships. International, and particularly U.S. support for civilian authority over all institutions of government, including the security forces, is critically important to this process. Unfortunately, U.S. policy towards Guatemala appears to be motivated more by the Reagan Administration's attempts to undermine President Cerezo's "active neutrality" in the United States's war against Nicaragua than by a desire to strengthen his control over a still-powerful military. The Reagan Administration has conducted a public relations campaign to refurbish the military's appalling human rights record, but it has not invited President Cerezo to visit the White House. It has provided direct assistance to the Guatemalan security forces, and it has let it be known that more aid might be forthcoming if the government abandons its neutrality on Nicaragua. It has professed support for civilian democratic government in

Guatemala, but it has sought to explain away the incapacity of the civilian government to make institutional headway in establishing the rule of law.

a. Reagan Administration Reporting on Human Rights in Guatemala -- The Background: The Reagan Administration's public position on human rights in Guatemala is that political abuses have all but ended since President Cerezo took office. The State Department desk officer on Guatemala has gone so far as to assert publicly that "there has not been a single clear-cut case of political killing" under the civilian government. This denial of human rights violations by the Guatemalan security forces is consistent with the Reagan Adminstration's defense of the military under previous governments. Reviewing the record, we find that the Reagan Administration failed to condemn gross violations by Presidents Lucas, Rios, and Mejia while each in turn held office. At times, it praised their performance on human rights. Only when each successive military dictator left office was his human rights record criticized for purposes of favorably comparing his successor. Thus in July 1981, a State Department spokesman cited "positive developments" during the Lucas Garcia regime, including "a very comprehensive program to try to improve the lot of the Guatemalan Indians who live in some of the more backward areas" and praised the army for "taking care to protect innocent bystanders" in the counterinsurgency war. When Lucas was replaced by General Efrain Rios Montt, the Reagan Administration criticized the Lucas Government and praised Rios for a "dramatic decline" in human rights abuses and for demonstrating a "commitment to positive change and new opportunity in Guatemala." President

82

Reagan himself publicly embraced President Rios as "a man of great personal integrity and commitment" who was getting a "bum rap" by human rights critics. When Rios was replaced by General Oscar Humberto Mejia Victores in August 1983, the Administration lauded him in turn for curbing violations committed by Rios -- violations which the Administration did not acknowledge during President Rios's tenure in office. The State Department reported "a dramatic decline in reports of violence and political deaths in the countryside" and noted that "Democracy is on track in Guatemala... the overall human rights situation in Guatemala has also improved, and the trends are encouraging." (See the Americas Watch Report, "Guatemala Revised: How the Reagan Administration Finds 'Improvements' in Human Rights in Guatemala," September 1985.)

b. Reagan Administration Reporting in 1986: The Reagan Administration continues to report human rights improvements in Guatemala. In a June 6, 1986 certification report required by law as a prerequisite for military aid to Guatemala, the State Department claimed that "Since January 1986 the level of disappearances and politically-motivated killings has dropped significantly... Since the inauguration, abductions and politically-motivated killings have further dropped to a monthly average of 10 and 12 respectively."

Though there have been reductions in human rights abuses, including an end to the army's practice of mass murder in the countryside and assassination of political opponents in the city, it is *not* the case that there have been no political killings and disappearances since President Cerezo took office. Nor can it safely be said that the monthly figures for such violations

83

number 10 and 12 respectively. Because no human rights monitoring organizations have been able to operate within Guatemala, all reporting on the actual numbers of human rights abuses is conjectural. The State Department's Guatemala desk officer claims that the U.S. Embassy has a "data base" on Guatemalan human rights abuses which includes information from 17 different sources. Yet none of these sources conducts systematic interviews with witnesses, takes testimony from family members, or investigates abuses where they occur. In the coming year it is hoped that the Catholic Church's newly-formed human rights monitoring office will be able to play such a role. For 1986 however, the Embassy had to rely upon the same statistics available to the Americas Watch -- those published by the Guatemalan press.

Though the Guatemalan press reports on many violent crimes, it rarely indicates which may be political and almost never attributes blame to the armed forces. This is hardly surprising as most of the information on such crimes is provided to the press by the police and the armed forces. As noted in Chapter VIII, Freedom of Expresion and Association, there is very little press investigation of crimes; indeed, there is little travel of any sort by the press outside Guatemala city to remote rural areas where many abuses take place.

Though the Guatemalan press is not a useful source of information about the *numbers* of political killings, press reports on the circumstances of certain cases provide some indication of politically-motivated violence. For example, the Guatemalan newspapers frequently report on bodies that appear with signs of mutilation and torture, or with their hands tied behind their backs -- the *modus operandi* of political murder in Guatemala

84

for many years. (The Reagan Administration generally ignores such circumstantial evidence in its own reports on human rights in Guatemala.) In other instances, newspapers have reported denunciations by witnesses to violence. For example, *La Hora* of June 30, 1986 published a denunciation by church workers from the town of El Estor in Izabal on the disappearance of eight men and the killing of a number of women and children. (See Chapter VI, Military Violations in Rural Areas.) This account was later supported by the office of the papal nuncio in Guatemala City. The killings and disappearances of displaced persons regarded by the army as "subversive" should be categorized as politically-motivated.

Other reported cases are not obviously political, in the sense that the victims are not regarded as "subversive" or even as politically active, but constitute something other than common crime. One such case that we looked into during our November mission was the October 25, 1986 disappearance of an attorney, Dora Alicia de Lara. (See Chapter IV, Political Killings and Disappearances). Mrs. Lara, who was not politically active, was litigating a case involving a land title dispute against a captain and a colonel in the army. Family and friends attribute her disappearance to members of the armed forces who wanted to end her involvement in the litigation; they have accused the police of deliberately bungling an investigation and of covering up the crime. Such abuses by members of the armed forces -- not for ideological reasons but rather to settle personal scores -- might be considered "political violence" in the sense that the perpetrators act with no fear of apprehension and prosecution. Though it is impossible to tell what proportion of the "common" crimes reported in the Guatemalan press are actually committed by members of the security forces, civil patrols, or civilian-military commissioners, many Guatemalans, including members of the Congressional Human Rights Commission, told us that these forces continue to commit violent acts with impunity under the civilian government. The United States Embassy does not categorize such killings and disappearances as "political."

An episode that reflects, in microcosm, the lengths to which the State Department will go in attempting to deny human rights abuses began with an op-ed article published in *The New York Times* on July 14, 1986 by anthropologist Beatriz Manz. In the course of a visit to Guatemala City in June, Manz witnessed the execution-style killing of a young man on the street in the downtown business section at an early evening hour. Her article in the *Times* described the killing and noted that the Guatemalan police did not attempt to investigate it and did not report it to the Guatemalan press. The failure to report it was significant because press accounts, derived from information provided to the press by the police, are the main source of data on killings in Guatemala.

On July 29, Assistant Secretary of State Elliott Abrams wrote a letter to the editor of the *Times* criticizing Manz's article. According to Abrams, "despite Manz's claims to the contrary, the murder was reported in the Guatemalan press (*La Prensa*, June 27)." Abrams went on to say that Manz should be "more objective in her reporting."

Abrams' letter was not published by the *Times*, but a copy was forwarded to Americas Watch by the State Department in response to a query about the Department's comments about Manz's article. Accordingly, on September 4, Aryeh Neier, Vice Chairman of Americas Watch -- who was in Guatemala with

Manz when the murder she witnessed took place, and accompanied her to the hospital where the body was taken -- wrote to Abrams in response to his letter. Neier pointed out that there is no *La Prensa* in Guatemala and, presumably, Abrams intended to refer to *Prensa Libre*. However, Americas Watch had not found a reference to the murder in *Prensa Libre* of June 27, or in any other paper for that date. Neier asked Abrams for a copy of the article to which he referred.

Abrams did not respond. Subsequently, however, Americas Watch obtained a complete copy of *Prensa Libre* for June 27 and confirmed that no article about the murder appeared. On the other hand, that paper did have a funeral notice for the young man who was killed that did not mention that he had been murdered or any other relevant facts. Accordingly, Neier wrote to Secretary of State George Shultz on October 6 pointing out that Abrams had apparently furnished misleading information to the *Times* and, at the least, owed an apology to Beatriz Manz for characterizing her as not "objective in her reporting."

On November 3, an aide to Secretary Shultz, Patrick Fitzgerald, responded to Neier for the Department of State. Fitzgerald wrote that, "Although you are correct in asserting the Guatemalan press did not report the crime in the form of a news story, the death was in the press in the form of an obituary notice on June 27." Neier responded on November 6, pointing out that Fitzgerald's letter "suggests that the State Department considers it proper to provide such misleading information to the press. Is that what you intended?" There was no answer to that letter.

The State Department's reporting on Guatemalan human rights is also flawed by its failure to speak frankly about the military's continued control over civilians in the rural areas. The civil patrols are particularly important because the U.S. Congress has insisted that military aid to Guatemala be conditioned upon eliminating forced recruitment into the patrols. In its June 1986 certification to Congress, the Administration stated that "There is no evidence that the Guatemalan government is forcibly conscripting persons into the patrols or holding them there against their will. Nonetheless, undoubtedly many patrol members believe it prudent to participate in village patrols because of peer pressure." The reference to "peer pressure" does not adequately convey the reality of the military's continued occupation of the countryside, where a majority of the military commanders remain in place from past regimes. Guatemalan church sources note that, though it is indeed the case that civil patrols have actually been dismantled in some areas, patrols still serve as a means of social control in other areas; and many of the 800,000 or so current patrollers still endure onerous unpaid civil patrol duty for fear of retribution from local military commanders. (See Chapter V, Counter-Insurgency).

The Reagan Administration's insistence that killings and kidnappings are "common" criminal acts is the 1986 version of its assertion during previous governments that it was impossible to attribute responsibility for most killings and disappearances in Guatemala. By exonerating the military from responsibility for the wave of violence that has swept Guatemala City since President Cerezo took office, the Reagan Administration does a disservice to those in President Cerezo's government attempting to bring the military under civilian control. President Cerezo himself has acknowledged publicly that he does not possess complete control over the government; it does not help him to have the most powerful external force simultaneously insisting that he is fully in control; that abuses by the armed forces are at an end; and that abuses actually committed by the military were committed by common criminals. The invocation of that formula to explain the continuing violence in Guatemala enhances President Cerezo's difficulty in establishing control by depriving him of his means of securing actual changes in the practices of the military; his ability to see to it that U.S. funding is only used to reward actual improvements; his ability to remove and punish those continuing to commit abuses; and his ability to see to it that the reputation of the armed forces is commensurate with its actual performance.

c. U.S. Military and Police Assistance: The Reagan Administration repeatedly proposed that Congress authorize direct military aid to the Guatemalan armed forces during the past six years, though Congress did not approve aid until 1985 due to Guatemala's poor human rights record. Aside from going to Congress for direct aid, according to the General Accounting Office, export licenses were granted by the executive branch for sales of military equipment totaling $31,807 in 1982, $247,010 in 1983, $116,776 in 1984 and $374,207 in 1985 in spite of legislation prohibiting the granting of export licenses for commercial sales of military equipment to governments "engaged in a pattern of gross violations of internationally-recognized human rights." This does not include such equipment as trucks and jeeps which the Reagan Administration reclassified in 1981 as other than security assistance in order to license their sale to Guatemala.

Anticipating the Reagan Administration's eagerness to re-establish a military relationship with the Guatemalan armed forces after the election of a civilian government, Congress attached a series of conditions to legislation authorizing military aid for Guatemala. They included a requirement that the civilian president himself request the aid, and that the U.S. State Department certify that human rights conditions in Guatemala had improved demonstrably. On May 22, 1986, *The Washington Post* reported that President Cerezo had sent a letter to President Reagan requesting "less than $1 million" of the $10 million military aid authorized by Congress. Yet the Reagan Administration informed Congress that it would provide Guatemala with $5 million in military aid grants. The executive branch has assured the Congress that President Cerezo requested $5 million (rather than the $1 million cited in *The Washington Post*) but did not make his letter of request available. Some Congressional observers fear that the Administration has urged the Guatemalan military to pressure President Cerezo to request larger amounts, notwithstanding his express desire to receive the aid in small increments in response to actual human rights improvements by the armed forces. (Though the Administration announced its intention to provide $5 million in military aid to Guatemala, *The Washington Post* reported on December 16, 1986 that because of huge budget cuts in overall foreign aid levels, Guatemala actually only received $2 million in military aid.)

Top civilian officials in Cerezo's government have reported that the United States Embassy in Guatemala is pressuring the Guatemalan military to abandon its neutral position in the Nicaraguan war in exchange for higher military aid levels. In a meeting in November, President Cerezo himself told our delegation that he would not seek large amounts of military assistance from the United States. Yet in the same week, *The*

Washington Post reported that General Hector Alejandro Gramajo, the armed forces chief of staff, would like $50 to $60 million in U.S. military aid next year, which represents a tenfold increase over this year's aid. On the other hand, President Cerezo was quoted as saying that "the armed forces are not pressing for more [aid]. This shows they are committed to the democratic project here." More recently, President Cerezo has said that Guatemala received only $2 million in military aid rather than the $5 million originally requested by the State Department because the United States is pressuring "to have my government drop its policy of active neutrality." President Cerezo went on to say that "We believe President Reagan will correct this decision. If he does not, we will have to intrepret this as a means of pressuring Guatemala into supporting U.S. policy in Central America." (*Prensa Libre*, January 20, 1987).

The Guatemalan army prevailed over the guerrilla insurgency without U.S. assistance. Accordingly, the Reagan Administration's effort to provide increased military aid is not a response to a security threat. It is, rather, an attempt to win the support of the Guatemalan military for the Reagan Administration's geopolitical designs in Central America, despite President Cerezo's repeatedly expressed wishes to remain neutral. The United States should not force military aid on President Cerezo nor attempt to create divisions between him and his armed forces. U.S. military aid should be conditioned, as is required by law, upon human rights improvements, including complete civilian control over all elements of the armed forces and an end to involuntary participation in the civilian patrols.

The U.S. has also initiated a program of police assistance to Guatemala under the auspices of the Anti-Terrorism Assistance

91

Program. This program will train Guatemalan police officers in the U.S. and provide $150,000 to $200,000 worth of radios and other equipment.

This is not the first time the U.S. has provided assistance to the Guatemalan police. Guatemala received $5.6 million in police aid in the 1960s and 1970s under the Public Safety Program, including radios, weapons, and special assistance in establishing a police intelligence center in Guatemala City. A 1967 report from the U.S. Agency for International Development on U.S. police assistance to Guatemala somewhat vaguely acknowledged that police were engaged in extrajudicial killing, stating that "there did appear to be some organizations in existence that bypassed the courts in impressing suspected guerrillas and their supporters of the error of their ways." A 1971 Senate Foreign Relations Committee report on the aid program was more direct, stating, that "... the Guatemalan police operate without any effective political or judicial restraints, and how they use the equipment and techniques which are given them through the public safety program is quite beyond U.S. control ... the U.S. is politically identified with police terrorism."

The State Department justifies its current assistance to the police on the grounds that the police are unable to carry out investigations of crime or human rights violations because of their lack of training and equipment. However, the Guatemalan government has sought and is receiving generous assistance for their police forces from a number of other countries, including West Germany, France, Spain, and Venezuela. Given the United States's role in establishing and supporting Guatemalan police intelligence services which came to be wholly associated with death squad violence, the U.S. has a case to make in establishing the legitimacy of renewed assistance. At the very least, the U.S. should refrain from again assisting those forces until such time as all elements who have engaged in abuses in the past have been purged from the institution; until those who engaged in murder have been investigated and prosecuted; and until systematic police violence and corruption has ended.

XI. GUATEMALA AND EUROPE: REMARKS BY THE BRITISH PARLIAMENTARY HUMAN RIGHTS GROUP

a. European Political Attitudes and Assistance to Guatemala: When President Cerezo took office in January 1986 he faced a formidable task. Any attempt to establish democratic institutions and respect for human rights in Guatemala after years of brutal military governments was bound to be immensely difficult. So far the President has not been notably successful.

As we have described elsewhere in this report, there has been a considerable decrease in the numbers of human rights abuses, as compared with the appallingly high numbers of the recent past, but they have not been eliminated. Even more worrying, perhaps, is the fact that, so far, such little headway seems to have been made in establishing the precedence of civilian authority over military power.

Some analysts argue that the President missed an opportunity to move decisively against the military immediately after the election which brought him to office, with a huge popular mandate. Whatever the truth of this, it is clear that if there is to be any chance of successfully restoring democracy in Guatemala, international encouragement for the strengthening of civilian control over the institutions of the state will be a crucial factor. Europe has an important role to play in this process.

There is little doubt that the governments of several member countries of the European Economic Community have been impressed by the foreign policy of President Cerezo during his first year of office. They are particularly interested in the Guatemalan government's stance of "active neutrality" in the Central American regional situation. The policy, which is under pressure from the United States Administration and also possibly from elements within the Guatemalan military, won praise at the United Nations, where President Cerezo spoke immediately before a much-publicised visit to Europe in October 1986. The visit was undertaken to persuade Western European governments that Guatemala deserved to receive large amounts of economic aid, following the establishment of a civilian presidency.

President Cerezo certainly scored a personal success in Europe. He was able to secure pledges of almost US$300 million in loans and credits, including US$58.4 million in grants from various European sources. The breakdown is:

Credits and Loans			Grants		
Italy	US$100	million	Italy	US$46	million
W. Germany*	70	million	W. Germany	5	million
France	50	million	France	5.7	million
Spain	2.7	million	Holland	1.5	million
Belgium	1.25	million			
EEC	1.5	million			

Commercial Credit

Banco de la Union Europea   US$ 10 million
(Source: INFORPRESS CENTROAMERICANA)

The policy of 'active neutrality' deserves support from Europe. It is a crucial element in the attempt to find a political solution to the conflicts in Central America. European aid to Guatemala could have an important role in connection with this. Such aid will be a factor in reducing, to some extent at least, Guatemala's dependence on economic assistance from the United States and thus perhaps reducing the vulnerability of 'active neutrality' as a foreign policy option of the Cerezo Government.

However, the granting of aid from Europe places a great burden of responsibility on the donor nations, both individually and within the European Community as a whole. It will be vital for Europeans to maintain special vigilance towards developments in Guatemala, especially in the area of human rights.

While he was in Europe, President Cerezo was at pains to promote an image of his presidency as marking a sharp break with the recent brutal past of his country. Many Guatemalans, however, agree with an earlier admission of the President that he controls only about 30% of power and argue that much of the rest remains with the armed forces. This is borne out by the lack of significant progress in dismantling the system erected by the military to ensure its continuing control, before handing over the office of the president to a civilian. Elsewhere in this report we describe the situation of the Inter-institutional Coordination Committees, renamed Councils of Development, model villages and development poles and the civil patrol system. Furthermore,

97

the government's failure to investigate past human rights abuses, and the alarmingly high, and apparently increasing, incidence of murder and disappearance, is a disquieting indication that the military's traditional system of dealing with opponents remains intact and can be intensified whenever the armed forces deem it necessary. President Cerezo admitted as much in his November meeting with Americas Watch and the British Parliamentary Human Rights Group.

President Cerezo's position is that any progress towards real change in Guatemala will, of necessity, be very slow. He explained to our delegation that if he attempts to force the pace he risks a reaction from the military, even the possibility of a coup. He recognizes that this will be a long process, probably even beyond the term of his office, but he maintains that if he is to have any chance of consolidating civilian power against the armed forces then this is the only feasible policy.

This raises important issues for European aid donors. If President Cerezo's strategy is to have any chance of success then international support for the policy is important and Europe can make an important contribution but there are great dangers. It would be a tragedy if there was any attempt from within Europe to emulate the Reagan Administration's consistent efforts to explain away or to distort the reality of the Guatemalan situation. The inability, so far, of the civilian administration to control the armed forces and to establish its own authority over the state is a factor which must govern European support for, and economic assistance to, the Cerezo government. For this reason, aid to Guatemala from Europe should keep pace with improvements in the human rights situation and criteria should be established for measuring this.

The record of the first year is not good, and this makes it essential that the most stringent conditions and the strictest monitoring procedures are attached to all European aid packages, whether bilateral or from the Community as a whole. In the case of certain categories of aid, e.g. police aid and rural development projects, it will be even more important for European governments to ensure that the resources they provide are not used to finance repressive action against the population or for counter-insurgency purposes.

In monitoring the situation the proposed Procurator's office will be an obvious and important point of contact for European aid donors -- provided that it receives the official support necessary to ensure its effective working as a barometer of human rights improvements. However, it will perhaps be even more important to establish contact with the new human rights office of the Catholic Church in Guatemala. This independent agency will, it is hoped, be in a position to provide unbiased and well researched information which will be invaluable to all those with a genuine desire to assist the building of democracy and respect for human rights in Guatemala.

In the past many European governments have expressed their anxiety about the human rights situation in Guatemala through such institutions as the United Nations Human Rights Commission. There has been consistent support from various European members of the United Nations for a series of successful Resolutions condemning Guatemala's human rights record; a number of the Resolutions have been sponsored and introduced by European delegations. It is important that Europe's concern about Guatemala continues to be demonstrated through organisations such as the United Nations, but it is equally important that the opportunity offered by President Cerezo's approach to Europe is recognised and acted upon. European governments now have a chance to bring direct influence to bear on future developments in Guatemala. That influence should be used to promote the establishment of a truly democratic society, where people can live free from fear, under the rule of law.

b. Britain and Guatemala: Traditionally the relationship between Britain and Guatemala has centered on the question of Guatemala's territorial ambitions towards its neighbour Belize, a former British colony. Belize became independent on September 21, 1981 and since that date the British government has insisted publicly that the resolution of the dispute is a matter for Guatemala and Belize. This is contrary to the official policy of Guatemala, which has never recognised Belize as an independent entity. Nevertheless, Britain has continued to play a leading role in diplomatic and political moves designed to find a solution to the problem.

It now seems likely that renewed efforts are underway to resolve the dispute. The Guatemalan government has announced its intention of holding a plebiscite to endorse diplomatic recognition of Belize, despite continuing opposition from some military and right wing elements in Guatemala. In the meantime full diplomatic relations between Britain and Guatemala, broken over the question of Belize in 1963, were renewed on December 27, 1986. There will be an exchange of ambassadors in the near future.

We welcome the restoration of diplomatic relations. We believe that the establishment of a British diplomatic mission to

Guatemala is of great importance, especially in connection with the role it will play in the definition of British policy towards Guatemala, at this crucial time in the country's history. The British Embassy's monitoring of the situation will not only be of importance in the elaboration of the British attitude towards the country but will also be influential, through Britain's membership in the European Economic Community, on the development of thinking at a European level.

It will be most important that the British ambassador creates a mechanism through which developments in the political situation, particularly as regards human rights can be monitored very efficiently. This should be an absolute pre-condition for any aid or trading agreements between Britain and Guatemala. In view of the offer of a small aid program to Guatemala made by British Minister for Foreign and Commonwealth Affairs, Lady Young, during the meeting in Guatemala of Central American and European Community Foreign Ministers the 9th and 10th of February, 1987, this is now an urgent priority. In respect to aid from Britain it is most desirable that close contact is maintained between British Embassy staff and those British non-governmental organisations, with long experience of conditions in the country, who are presently operating development programmes in Guatemala.

This will be particularly important in connection with projects where aid could be manipulated to impede the process of democracy. The expertise and advice of agency staff will be of invaluable assistance in the evaluation of this kind of project. It may also be considered wise to channel some potential financing of projects directly through non-governmental organisations in co-funding arrangements. This would have the benefit of ensuring a constant supervision by the field officers and project workers of the non-governmental agencies, and could be an important safeguard against the misuse of British government money.

The present climate of renewed friendship with Guatemala presents Britain with a unique chance to play a role in influencing the future destiny of the country. The British government should take this responsibility very seriously and make every effort to ensure that British policy towards Guatemala is based on principles which encourage the flourishing of freedom and democracy. There will inevitably be strong pressure from the United States for British policy to follow that of its major ally, and it will be argued that Guatemala is relatively peripheral to British interests. Nevertheless it would be disastrous if Britain's policy towards Guatemala had the effect of assisting present United States government strategy, which is described in this report, especially the attempt to involve the armed forces of Guatemala in the Reagan Administration's geo-political plans. The policy can only reduce any chance President Cerezo may have of prevailing over the Guatemalan armed forces, and that can only worsen the conditions of the majority of the population. It is their interests, we suggest, which should guide the formulation of British policy.

APPENDIX A

Chronology of a Disappearance

The following is a chronology of a disappearance of a student, Luis Fernando de la Roca Elias, which occurred in 1985. The abduction of Luis Fernando was unusually well-documented because a guard at the family's home recorded the license plate numbers of two vehicles which took him. The vehicles were later traced to the Guatemalan military and police. The following chronology summarizes the family's many efforts to force the Guatemalan Supreme Court to establish Luis Fernando's whereabouts, investigate the ownership of the vehicles, and, finally, to prosecute those military officials responsible. The virtual powerlessness of the court to force the military to produce the disappeared student or even carry out a serious investigation of his abduction and disappearance is a sobering commentary on the tenuousness of civilian authority in Guatemala generally.

"General Justo Rufino Barrios" is the name of the Central Military Barracks in Guatemala City.

* * * *

September 9, 1985: Luis Fernando de la Roca Elias doesn't appear at his home at the end of the day.

September 10, 11, 12, 1985: The relatives of Luis Fernando look for him in hospitals and detention centers.

September 12, 1985: At 11:30 am several vehicles with armed men arrive in front of the entrance to the condominium "Residencias Exclusivas Mariscal" at 71-12 14th Avenue of Zone 11 in Guatemala City, the home of Luis Fernando. The license plate of the vehicle is P-253217, as recorded on the sign-in sheet by the building's guard.

The house is searched, and Luis Fernando's mother, Rosa Elvira Elias Alburez, is told that Luis Fernando is imprisoned at Precinct 20 of the National Police, and that they are searching for arms. The group included several men with radio transmitters.

At 1:20 pm armed men again enter the condominium in the same vehicle and with another vehicle, license plate number P-75177. Luis Fernando is taken from this vehicle, tied and bleeding, and brought into the house, which is again searched. Luis Fernando is then taken away in one vehicle and his mother and a little granddaughter are taken away in the other vehicle. The mother is blindfolded and driven for half an hour in the outskirts of the city. The car is stopped, her blindfold is removed, and she sees Luis Fernando being beaten in the other vehicle. She and the child are taken back to the condominium.

She does not see Luis Fernando again.

September 12, 1985: The sister of Luis Fernando, Julia Eloisa de la Roca Elias, files a *habeas corpus* writ in the Supreme Court on behalf of her abducted brother, and asking the court for a preventive order to protect herself and her mother. The writ includes a description of events and the license plate numbers of the vehicles.

The Supreme Court orders the government to produce Luis Fernando, and also orders a report from the Transit Department of the National Police regarding the license plates in question and the institution or person they belong to. The report reveals nothing.

September 18, 1985: Another *habeas corpus* writ is introduced by the family at the Supreme Court, including an affidavit from the security guard who recorded the license plates of the vehicles and photographs of the vehicles' tire marks in the yard.

December 20, 1985: Report #15441 is filed with the Secretariat of the Supreme Court of Justice dated October 16, 1985 from the "Department of Tax on the Use of Services and Commercial Activities, Automotive Tax Division of the General Office of Internal Revenue of the Ministry of Public Finances." The report states that according to their files, license P-253217 was assigned to the General Barracks "General Justo Rufino Barrios" of the Army and license P-75177 to the Ministry of Defense.

January 2, 1986: The Supreme Court of Justice declares the *habeas corpus* writs on behalf of Luis Fernando invalid and rules that in view of the October 16 report, (cited above) the military court of the Central Military Zone "General Justo Rufino Barrios" Barracks should carry out the inquiry.

January 8, 1986: Luis Fernando's mother introduces another *habeas corpus* writ and specifically names Head of State Oscar Humberto Mejia Victores, and General Hector Alejandro Gramajo Morales, the chief of the "General Barracks General Justo Rufino Barrios". In response, the Court appoints the Seventh Judge of the First Instance to investigate the "General Barracks General Justo Rufino Barrios." The job was undertaken by a woman who described the negative results of her investigation and the fact that she was treated with contempt during her inquiries.

January 10, 1986: Luis Fernando's mother asks for a new hearing and requests that General Gramajo Morales be questioned about the licensed vehicles. The Court did not respond to this motion.

February 5, 1986: Another *habeas corpus* writ is introduced by the family.

February 6, 1986: This is the last day to produce Luis Fernando, as designated by the Court in the most recent *habeas corpus* it considered. The Court's order is disobeyed.

In view of the apparent cover-up by the military authorities of the kidnapping, the family requests that the Supreme Court of Justice continue its inquiry into the location and ownership of the vehicles, and prosecute those responsible for the abduction.

106

The Supreme Court declines to prosecute, and orders that the Sixth Criminal Court of First Instance make further inquiries.

February 14, 1986: General Jaime Hernandez Mendez, Minister of Defense, informs the court in document #02151 that the license plate P-253217 had been assigned to the "Service of War Material" of the Army and that plate P-75177 had been assigned to the "Command of the Itinerant Military Police". The report further stated that neither sets of plates were in use on September 9 and 12 because they had both been "stolen" by "unknown perpetrators", and that "through confidential reports" they had the information that these plates were being used "by members of subversive delinquency".

April 17, 1986: Luis Fernando's mother, after receiving no information from the previous habeus corpus writs, submits a memorandum to the court and insists that the kidnapping of her son be investigated and that as a pertinent part of the investigation a report be requested from the General Command of the National Police as to whether and on what date any action had been requested to stop the vehicles with plates P-253217 and P-75177, and whether in the General Command of the Police any warrant to detain such vehicles had been received.

April 28, 1986: Document #1706.86 is submitted by the General Command of the National Police informing the court that the cooperation of the police had not been requested to detain the vehicles and that there were no warrants issued against these vehicles. The report was signed by Colonel of Infantry, Alberto Pinto Recinos.

June 20, 1986: The families submitted another memo to the court in response to the report mentioned above again asking that all appropriate steps be employed to locate the kidnapped person and requesting prosecution of the President of the Republic, the Minister of Defense, and the chief of the "Barracks General Justo Rufino Barrios".

July 7, 1986: The family, having received no notification from its recent submissions, asks the court to notify them about the results of its latest *habeas corpus* writ.

July 12, 1986: There is no sign that the court will take further action in the case of Luis Fernando de la Roca Elias.

MEMBERS AND STAFF
OF THE
AMERICAS WATCH

Members

Orville H. Schell, Chairman; Aryeh Neier, Vice Chairman; Peter Bell, Robert L. Bernstein, Albert Bildner, Abraham Brumberg, Paul Chevigny, Dorothy Cullman, Drew S. Days III, Patricia Derian, Adrian DeWind, Stanley Engelstein, Tom J. Farer, Wendy Gimbel, Robert Goldman, Jack Greenberg, Wade J. Henderson, Alice Henkin, Anne Johnson, Russell Karp, Stephen Kass, Marina Kaufman, Jeri Laber, Margaret Lang, Marshall Meyer, John B. Oakes, Michael Posner, Bruce Rabb, Jeanne Richman, Sanford Solender, Giorgio Solimano, M.D., George Soros, Alfred Stepan, Svetlana Stone, Rose Styron, Hector Timmerman, Jorge Valls, Lois Whitman

Staff

Aryeh Neier, Vice Chairman; Juan Mendez, Washington Office Director; Cynthia Brown, Associate Director; Holly Burkhalter, Washington Representative; Susan Osnos, Press Director; Jemera Rone, Counsel to Americas Watch; Mary Jane Camejo, Elizabeth Carr, Margaret Kennedy, Linda D. Long, Sue Nestel, Alita Paine, Karen Sirker, Karen Sorensen, Katherine Zill, Associates

Recent Publications of the
AMERICAS WATCH

Colombia:

"Human Rights in Colombia as President Barco Begins," September 1986, 68 pages. $7.00 ISBN 0-938579-26-6

"The Central-Americanization of Colombia?" January 1986, 146 pages. $8.00 (AW44) ISBN 0-938579-01-0

Cuba:

"Twenty Years and Forty Days: Life in A Cuban Prison," April 1986, 125 pages. $8.00 (AW55) ISBN 0-938579-18-5

El Salvador:

"Land Mines in El Salvador and Nicaragua - The Civilian Victims, December 1986, 117 pages. $8.00 ISBN 0-938579-29-0

"Settling into Routine: Human Rights in Duarte's Second Year," May 1986, 162 pages. $10.00 (AW56) ISBN 0-938579-19-3

"Managing the Facts: How the Administration Deals with Reports of Human Rights Abuses in El Salvador," December 1985, 42 pages. $4.00 (AW45)

"The Continuing Terror," September 1985, 156 pages. $10.00
(AW46) ISBN 0-938579-02-9

Guatemala:

"Civil Patrols in Guatemala," August 1986, 80 pages. $6.00
(AW57) ISBN 0-938579-20-7

"Guatemala: The Group for Mutual Support," December 1985, 57
pages. Photographs. $10.00 (AW47) ISBN 0-938579-06-1

"Guatemala Revised: How the Reagan Adminstration Finds
'Improvements' in Human Rights in Guatemala," September 1985,
20 pages. $3.00 (AW48)

Haiti:

"Haiti: Duvalierism Since Duvalier," October 1986, 75 pages.
$7.00 (ISBN 0-938579-28-2)

"Haiti: Human Rights Under Hereditary Dictatorship," October
1985, 33 pages. $4.00 (Americas Watch/National Coalition for
Haitian Refuges) (AW50)

Honduras:

"Human Rights in Honduras After General Alvarez," February 1986, 59 pages. $5.00 (AW69) ISBN 0-938579-21-5

Jamaica

"Human Rights in Jamaica," September 1986, 64 pages. $6.00 ISBN 0-938579-27-4

Nicaragua:

"Human Rights in Nicaragua 1986," February 1986, 175 pages. $8.00 ISBN 0-938579-30-4.

"Land Mines in El Salvador and Nicaragua - The Civilian Victims, December 1986, 117 pages. $8.00 ISBN 0-938579-29-0.

"Human Rights in Nicaragua 1985-1986," March 1986, 154 pages. $8.00 (AW61) ISBN 0-938579-22-3

"Human Rights in Nicaragua: Reagan, Rhetoric and Reality," July 1985, 91 pages. $8.00 (AW52) ISBN 0-938579-11-8

Paraguay:

"Paraguay: Latin America's Oldest Dictatorship Under Pressure" August 1986, 71 pages. $6.00 ISBN 0-938579-23-1

Peru:

"Human Rights in Peru After President Garcia's First Year," September 1986, 117 pages. $8.00 ISBN 0-938579-25-8

"A New Opportunity for Democratic Authority: Human Rights in Peru," September 1985, 43 pages. $5.00 (AW53) ISBN 0-938579-16-9 Available in Spanish

During the two decades preceding the
January 1986 inauguration of Vinicio
Cerezo as president, Guatemala
endured more sustained and pervasive
political violence than any other
country in the hemisphere, in the form
of death squad killings, rural massacres
and disappearances.

President Cerezo's inauguration raised
hopes for a new era in Guatemalan
history, an era of respect for human
dignity. However, despite President
Cerezo's personal commitment to
human rights, the situation in
Guatemala remains terrible.

Americas Watch and the British
Parliamentary Human Rights Group call
upon President Cerezo to expose the
abuses of the past, and to punish those
responsible. Without such an
accounting, these abuses can continue,
and the rule of law cannot be
established in Guatemala.

ISBN 0-938579-31-2